THE CELEBRITY COOKBOOK

By

Marla Brooks

A division of Shapolsky Publishers, Inc.

The Celebrity Cookbook

S.P.I. BOOKS
A division of Shapolsky Publishers, Inc.

ISBN 1-56171-041-5

For any additional information, contact:

S.P.I. BOOKS/Shapolsky Publishers, Inc.
136 West 22nd Street
New York, NY 10011
212/633-2022 / FAX 212/633-2123

Manufactured in the United States of America

10 9 8 7 6 5 4 3 2 1

DEDICATION

This book is dedicated to all the gourmands of the world . . . especially those friends and loved ones who helped me by testing the recipes. We've all gained a few pounds in the process, but it was well worth the effort!

ACKNOWLEDGEMENTS

A book such as this cannot be accomplished without the assistance of a great number of people. First of all, I would like to thank all the celebrity contributors. Without you, there would have been no book.

Secondly, to the following people, you all know what you did, but in case you've forgotten, call me up and ask. In the meantime, thanks to Charlie Brouyette, Stanley Ralph Ross, Todd Cote, Misak Barsamian, and Aram Barsamian.

A special thanks to Stephanie Waddick, who came over on a weekly basis with a hearty appetite, and a bottle of wine to wash all the recipes down.

Finally, to Rusty Brooks, otherwise known as Mom, it is true that certain traits are inherited. Unfortunately, your penchant for shopping somehow got lost in the DNA. I hate shopping, but you're not too crazy about cooking, so it balances out. Thanks for doing all the grocery shopping over these many months and for standing for hours at the checkout counter. I really do appreciate it, but please don't send me your chiropractor bills just yet. Let's see how the book does first.

Contents

INTRODUCTION

I really I didn't start out to do a book of this sort, I really didn't! It was one of those things that just happened. I was bored, and one afternoon I sat down to watch a cooking show on PBS, and the thought of writing a cookbook came to mind. I dismissed it at first as a folly, but the idea gnawed at the back of my mind for several days.

A week later, I had delusions of grandeur and thought it might be fun to try to do a cookbook. I had accumulated several recipes, and had a myriad of friends who were tremendous cooks, so I was sure I could put a nice, simple little book together and see what happened. On a lark, I thought of putting a celebrity chapter in the book, and went about mailing requests for recipes to several of my favorite people in the industry. I was absolutely positive that I would not receive any replies, but I thought "What the heck, let's try anyway..." and much to my surprise, I got a few responses. When I had a halfway decent book to try and sell, I contacted several publishers, to no avail until one day I got a letter in the mail from one stating that they were not interested in the book as it was, but if I could put together a book of celebrity recipes only, they might be interested. I worked a little harder, sent out a few more requests, got a few more replies, and then the publisher decided that it wasn't such a good idea, and told me to forget it. Well, one thing is for certain. If someone tells me to do something, I usually don't listen.

Thank goodness I didn't listen, because what you have before you is a cookbook like you've probably never seen. It incorporates recipes from a wide range of celebrities in almost every field imaginable. It's a potpourri of different foods, different cultures and different people. There's something here for everybody, whether you like to eat, or just like to know what others are enjoying.

PREFACE

There is no more enduring industry in the United States, nay, the world, then celebrity watching. This has been proven by the many tell-all books, slick magazines, supermarket gossip newspapers and videotrash television shows which chronicle their comings and goings, their follies and foibles and their general demeanor off the screen or out of the arenas, both sports and political. Despite what their millions of adoring fans might believe, these movers and shakers are just like everyone else in that they have to eat. Some of them actually enjoy eating, and a few of them even enjoy cooking.

In this book, Our Ms. Brooks has gathered a spectrum of recipes from various luminaries in all walks of life so it is entirely possible for a reader to sit down and watch their favorite personality on television while eating food that celebrity eats. Granted, there may be better things to do with one's time. Sex comes to mind, sleep is another suggestion, attending a sporting event might even take precedence but those aside, dining on a dish concocted and cherished by an idol could prove to be a pleasurable experience.

While foraging for recipes, Ms. Brooks also had many rejections. Those are duly noted and are sometimes even more informative as to the nature of the dignitary then the recipe. A few of the dishes are devilishly simple, some are unbelievably complicated but all are the real thing, not some fabrication invented by a free-lance recipe writer seeking to earn a few extra bucks.

We've tried a sampling of the dishes. A few were scrumptious and some made us wonder how these celebrities have survived on that kind of fare. Still, eating is, most of all, a matter of taste and you might savor what I didn't.

Brooks has done the world of dining a great service by taking celebrities out of the bedroom and into the kitchen, where most of them should have been anyhow.

Read. Enjoy. Cook. Eat. And if you get an upset stomach, don't blame Brooks. She merely gathered the recipes, the celebrities are the ones who conceived them.

Stanley Ralph Ross Hollywood, California
June 23, 1993

HINTS AND TIPS

Using fresh ingredients will make your food taste better, especially when using spices. One fresh clove of garlic is better than a whole bottle of garlic powder or (heaven forbid!) garlic *salt*. As a general rule, whether it be vegetables, herbs, or seasonings, try to use fresh. You'll notice a tremendous difference in the flavor. Also remember that fresh spices have a stronger flavor than those in jars, so use half as much fresh spices as you would the other kind.

Make sure your spice rack and cupboard is stocked with a good mix of basic ingredients, so you don't have to run out a buy something every time you pick up a new recipe. The very basic necessities to have on hand are as follows: Salt, black peppercorns, crushed red pepper flakes, cayenne pepper, a head of garlic, dried mustard, soy sauce, oregano, basil, thyme, rosemary, red pepper, tabasco, worcestershire sauce, dried mint, bay leaves, fresh nutmeg, cinnamon, pure vanilla extract, coriander, cumin, basil, cloves, paprika, ginger, celery seed, dill, sage, marjoram, cardamom, turmeric, and caraway seeds.

♣ ♣ ♣

It's a good idea to have more than one type of cooking oil on hand. I always keep olive oil, peanut oil and vegetable oil in my cupboard, and have found that I use them all equally. Toasted sesame oil is also a necessity in my kitchen, as I do a lot of oriental cooking, and toasted sesame oil really adds flavor! Make sure you give your oils the "sniff test" if they have been sitting around for a while on your shelf. They do go rancid after a while, and one sniff will let you know. If they do go bad, throw them away immediately!

Like oil, you should also have two or three vinegars hanging around. The most common are wine vinegar (white or red), cider vinegar, and white vinegar, although the fruited vinegars are a nice (but expensive, unless you make your own!) change of pace as well.

The most bothersome but necessary thing to keep on hand is a good stock. Many recipes call for chicken, beef or fish stock, and I never have one around. You can substitute canned stock, but it's not nearly as good as homemade.

♣ ♣ ♣

I was always annoyed when a recipe called for one teaspoon of tomato paste. It seemed horrible to me to open a whole can just to use one teaspoon, until I got a brainstorm that worked. After the can is open, put tablespoons of paste on wax paper and freeze them. As soon as they are frozen, transfer them to an airtight freezer container, and then use as needed.

♣ ♣ ♣

Most people don't like leftovers. I, however, find it a relief not to have to cook two days in a row. I was brought up to cook for a small army. Whether there were two or ten for dinner, there was always enough. I do draw the line if I have to eat the same thing more than twice. In that case, I freeze the remaining leftovers, and have them on a day I don't feel like cooking.

♣ ♣ ♣

The best way to peel a garlic clove is to smash it with a heavy object. I use my meat pounder. One good whack and the peel is off.

♣ ♣ ♣

Raisins, or any dried fruit that has been sitting in the fridge too long tend to dry out, even if well packaged. To plump them back up, place them in a bowl of water (or white wine, if you're adventurous) and in no time they will be back to normal.

♣ ♣ ♣

Kitchen knives need to be sharp at all times. If you can't cut through a ripe tomato without having to saw through it, your knives aren't sharp enough. Always keep a knife sharpener handy.

♣ ♣ ♣

When cooking rice, never peek at it during the cooking process. This will cause it to become sticky and pasty . . . which may be okay if you're making sushi, but just won't do if you are expecting to serve a light, fluffy rice side dish.

♣ ♣ ♣

Cooking is a chore *only* if you are not prepared. A well stocked kitchen, the proper cooking utensils, some basic knowledge and a little bit of planning in advance turns drudgery into fun.

♣ ♣ ♣

From time to time, recipes just don't work. Either you burn something, or you left out an ingredient, or your souffle fell. It happens to us all. If you are a beginner, don't let minor setbacks discourage you. The next time, it will work. Even Julia Child has her off days.

♣ ♣ ♣

Don't stick your nose up at something new if you haven't tried it. One of life's little pleasures is experimenting with new things. Back a few years, when sushi was all the rage, I thought I'd never be caught dead eating raw fish! Then, I tried it, and realized that it wasn't half bad. I had similar feelings about anchovies, brussel sprouts and chopped nuts on ice cream sundaes. These days, I can't eat a pizza without anchovies or a sundae without the nuts. As far as the brussel sprouts go, I'm still working on that one.

Salt is a necessity of life, but overdoing it isn't good. If you use a variety of spices in your cooking, you can nearly eliminate salt from your diet. I try not to cook with salt at all, and don't usually put out a salt shaker on the dinner table, unless it's specifically asked for. Food doesn't need salt to enhance the flavor. A good blend of seasonings will do that.

JOHNNY MATHIS' DUCK AND WILD RICE

Singer Johnny Mathis loves to cook. He learned how to cook from his parents, who worked for some of San Fransisco's wealthiest families.

Recently, Johnny rebuilt his kitchen, utilizing the latest cooking aids on the market. With all the modern luxuries, the kitchen still remains a comfortable spot where his dinner guests are encouraged to join him while he is preparing dinner.

2 or 3 ducks
Salt and pepper
1/2 cup chopped onion
1 sliced green pepper
2 or 3 celery stalks, cut
3 cups water

Preheat oven to 325 degrees. Clean ducks. Rub with salt and pepper. Place in baking pan, breast side up. Add onions, pepper slices, celery and water to the pan. Cover and bake at 325 degrees for 2 hours, or until ducks are tender. Baste occasionally. Serve on a bed of wild rice.

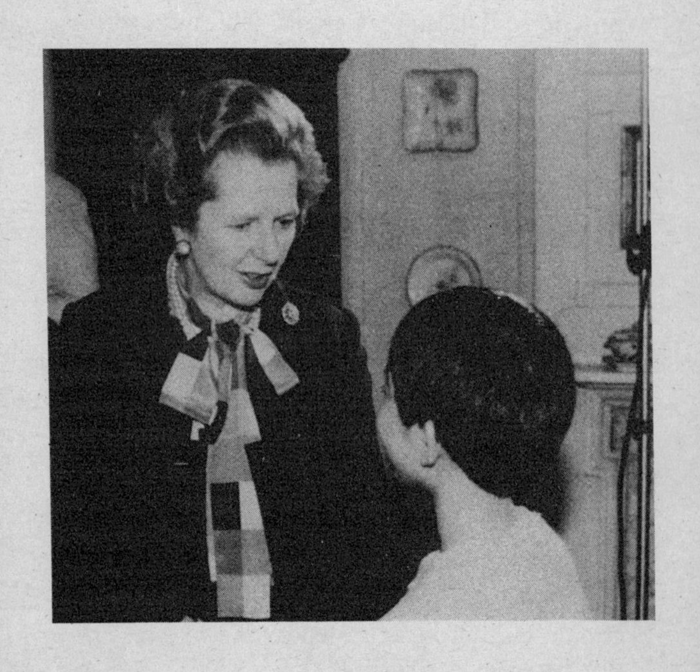

Former PRIME MINISTER MARGARET THATCHER'S COURGETTES MAISON

England's former Prime Minister is one of those people you really wouldn't expect to be standing over a hot stove, whipping up some tempting treat, but the following recipe proves that she knows her way around the kitchen as well as she did around Parliament!

4 courgettes (zucchini)
2-3 oz. butter
1 shallot
4 tomatoes
6 oz. prawns
1/2 pint mornay sauce
2 oz. cheese

Blanch courgettes whole until tender.

If large, finish the cooking wrapped in oiled greaseproof paper, and bake in moderate oven until tender.

Finely chop a shallot, soften in remaining butter, set aside.

When courgettes are tender cut off tops, or halve.

Scoop out flesh, mix it with shallot and tomatoes and season well.

Replace mixture in courgette skins. Place prawns on top.

Spoon over mornay sauce.

Add extra grated cheese–brown under grill.

MALCOLM FORBES' WARM PUMPKIN SOUP WITH SAUTEED LOBSTER

Financier Malcolm Forbes was probably one of the most well known people in the world, and one of the nicest. This was one of Mr. Forbes favorite recipes, prepared by his New York Chef.

4 cups pumpkin puree (fresh, frozen or canned)
2 cups chicken stock
1/4 cup molasses
1 Tablespoon sugar
1 dash each of allspice, cinnamon and nutmeg, salt and pepper
1/2 cup cream

Bring pumpkin puree and chicken stock to a boil. Add remaining ingredients and simmer for one-half hour. Serve warm with sauteed lobster and chopped parsley.

Sauteed Lobster

1 lb. lobster meat
1 teaspoon minced garlic
3 Tablespoons butter
Salt and pepper to taste

Melt butter in saute pan, and add lobster, garlic, salt and pepper. Toss for five minutes on medium heat. Serve warm on top of soup.

Serves 6

WILLIAM SHATNER'S CARROT VICHYSSOISE

Whether he is being beamed aboard the Starship Enterprise or hosting the hit TV show Rescue 911, a man has to eat . . . and in this case, William Shatner proves with this recipe that *REAL* men DO eat Vichyssoise!

2 handfuls peeled, diced potatoes
2 big handfuls sliced carrots
1 leek, sliced
3 cups vegetable stock
1 cup raw milk or 1/2 cup raw milk and cream

Combine first four ingredients in a saucepan. Bring to a boil. Reduce to a simmer for 25 to 30 minutes. Puree half of the vegetables and liquid in a blender. Empty into a bowl, add milk and a pinch of salt and pepper. Stir.

Serve cold in chilled bowls. Garnish with cold sliced scallions very sparingly.

Serves 3 - 4

ANTOINETTE IACOCCA'S ITALIAN MEATBALL SOUP

Italian cuisine is one of the most popular in the world, and so delicious, it's easy to see why. Lee Iacocca was very nice in taking time out to send his mother's delicious soup recipe.

1 stewing chicken or large fryer, about 4 lbs.
1 medium onion, quartered
1 large carrot, cut in chunks
1 large rib celery, cut in chunks
Cold water
Salt and freshly ground pepper to taste
1 lb. fine ground lean veal
1 large egg
1 1/2 Tablespoons grated Parmesan cheese
1/2 lb. small pasta squares
Additional grated Parmesan cheese

In large soup kettle or pot, combine chicken, onion, carrot and celery. Cover with cold water and bring to a boil. Season with salt and pepper to taste and simmer about two hours, until stock is reduced and chicken is very tender. Remove chicken, and strain stock into large bowl. Skim off most of fat on top. Remove meat from chicken bones. Shred enough chicken to make one cup; add to stock. (Save remaining chicken for another recipe, such as chicken salad.)

In medium bowl, combine veal, egg, Parmesan cheese and parsley; mix thoroughly and form into tiny meatballs about the size of a large marble.

Return de-fatted stock to pot and bring to a boil. Drop in meatballs and pasta squares and simmer 20 minutes. Ladle into soup bowls and sprinkle with grated Parmesan.

Makes about 8-10 servings.

SENATOR EDWARD M. KENNEDY'S NEW ENGLAND FISH CHOWDER

Senator Kennedy should be an expert in New England cuisine, and the following recipe makes that point perfectly clear.

2 lbs. fresh haddock
2 ounces salt pork, diced.
2 medium onions, sliced
1 cup chopped celery
4 large potatoes, diced
1 bay leaf, crumbled
4 cups milk
2 Tablespoons butter or margarine
1 teaspoon salt
Freshly ground black pepper to taste

Simmer haddock in 2 cups water for 15 minutes. Drain off and reserve the broth. Remove skin and bones from the fish. Saute the diced salt pork in a large pot until crisp. Remove salt pork and saute the onions in the pork fat until golden brown.

Add fish, celery, potatoes and bay leaf. Measure reserved fish broth, plus enough boiling water to make 3 cups liquid. Add to pot and simmer for 30 minutes. Add milk and butter and simmer for an additional 5 minutes, or until well heated.

Season with salt and pepper. Makes 8 servings.

ARNOLD PALMER'S HAWAIIAN MEAT BALLS

Obtaining a recipe for meat balls from one of America's foremost golfers is about the same as getting a recipe for spaghetti from Isaac Stern. It seems as though occupations and favorite foods go hand in hand. Thank you, Mrs. Palmer for sending this delicious recipe along!

1 1/2 pounds ground beef
2/3 cups cracker crumbs
1/2 cup chopped onion
2/3 cup evaporated milk
1 teaspoon seasoned salt
1/3 cup flour
3 Tablespoons shortening
Sweet and Sour Sauce (See recipe below)

Combine first 5 ingredients; mix lightly but thoroughly. Shape meat mixture into 30 balls. Roll in flour. Brown meatballs in shortening. Drain excess fat. Meanwhile, prepare Sweet-Sour Sauce. Pour over meatballs. Simmer, covered, for 15 minutes. Yield: 6 portions.

Sweet-Sour Sauce

1 can (13 1/2 oz.) pineapple chunks
2 Tablespoons cornstarch
1/2 cup vinegar
1/2 cup brown sugar

2 Tablespoons soy sauce
2 Tablespoons lemon juice
1 cup coarsely chopped green pepper
1 Tablespoon chopped pimento

Drain pineapple chunks; reserve pineapple. Measure syrup. Add water to make 1 cup liquid. Blend together pineapple liquid and cornstarch until smooth. Stir in next 4 ingredients and cook until thickened and clear. Add pineapple, green pepper, and pimento; mix well. Cover. Simmer over low heat for 15 minutes.

CONGRESSMAN FRED GRANDY'S ALMOND BREAD

Actor, turned Congressman Fred Grandy has come a long way from his role on The Love Boat to Iowa Congressman. Somewhere along the way, he has found time to hone his skills in the kitchen as well. Where does he find the time?

Set overnight:

One cup Grapenuts Cereal
3 cups cold milk

Beat Until Creamy:

2 eggs
1 Tablespoon butter
1 1/2 cups sugar

Cream into egg mixture:

1/2 pound almond paste

Sift together and then add to egg mixture alternately with milk mix:

3 cups flour
2 Tablespoons baking powder
1 Tablespoon baking soda

Bake at 350 degrees for one hour.
(Grease and flour pans heavily)

Freezes well!

CESAR ROMERO'S SPANISH RICE

Leading man Cesar Romero has a wonderful rice dish with a Spanish flair that would make a great accompaniment to any entree, north or south of the border.

1 cup washed rice
1/2 cup olive oil
3/4 cup boiling water
2 onions (sliced)
2 green peppers (sliced)
2 cups tomatoes (or tomato paste)
Salt and pepper to taste

Heat the olive oil, put the rice in the olive oil and stir until golden brown. Add the onions, peppers and tomatoes and mix together well. Then add water and let simmer for about 1/2 hour without stirring. Sprinkle parmesan cheese on top before serving.

Note: Another appetizing way to serve this dish is to put strips of bacon on top and bake in a slow oven until the bacon is crisp.

Serves 6 to 8 people. Not recommended for freezing.

JUSTIN WILSON'S DIRTY RICE

Cajun cook Justin Wilson cooks everything with aplomb, and this recipe for a rice side dish is wonderful, in spite of it's unappetizing name. Actually, it's so good, you may just want to serve it as a main course!

2 lbs. lean ground beef
2 lbs. lean ground pork
1 lb. chicken giblets (ground)
3 Tablespoons olive oil
2 cups finely chopped onion
2 cups finely chopped green onion
3/4 cup finely chopped bell pepper
1 cup finely chopped parsley
1 cup finely chopped celery
1/4 cup finely chopped garlic
1 teaspoon dried mint, crushed
1 teaspoon ground cayenne pepper
2 teaspoons Louisiana Hot Sauce
3 Tablespoons Lea & Perrin's Worcestershire sauce
4 teaspoons salt, or to taste
1 cup Chablis wine
Water
2 lbs. long grain rice, cooked separately

Mix all of the meats in a heavy pot on a medium heat burner. Add all the other ingredients, except for the rice. Cook on medium heat approximately 4 hours. Stir often. Add cooked rice, mixing thoroughly. Cook over low heat about 30 minutes.

This recipe is for a real party—12 to 30 people if you serve something else to eat.

STANLEY RALPH ROSS

STANLEY RALPH ROSS'S TOMATO AND EGG PIE

"Breakfast is my favorite meal, if it's done right. There is nothing like getting the day off to a good start and this is a dish I've been making for 30 years and it always works. This is the recipe for one serving, but you can add whatever you need to make it for more."

Stanley Ralph Ross
(Writer / producer / director / minister / lyricist / actor / very busy person / who, it would seem has very little time to cook!)

3 eggs
One can of peeled tomatoes or the equivalent in fresh tomatoes
Six ounces of mushrooms, canned or fresh, but fresh is preferred
One or two ounces freshly ground Parmesan cheese
Six strips of American, Jack, Swiss, Cheddar or whatever kind of cheese you like
Selected herbs and spices to your taste.

Take a medium sized frying pan (one that can be covered) and heat it on a low flame with two tablespoons of butter. Place tomatoes in the pan and allow them to simmer for two minutes. (You may also add the mushrooms, cut thinly, to the tomatoes.) Sprinkle with oregano or any other spices to your taste.

Cover the tomatoes with the cheese and let simmer for another minute. Break two or three eggs into the tomatoes, cover the pan and allow to simmer for another two minutes. Add thin strips of your favorite cheese in a cross-hatch fashion and again cover the pan and let simmer for another two minutes. Serve in frying pan or cut wedges and serve it along with fruit, bacon or other items as part of breakfast.

If prepared correctly, it will be about one inch high. There are those who like to add other vegetables, such as canned corn or string beans, but we prefer the more pristine recipe.

Total time: About 7 minutes, including preparation.

DONALD DUCK'S APPLESAUCE TOPPED HAM

As we all know, Donald Duck is a bit of a ham himself. The folks at the Walt Disney Company were kind enough to allow me to print my favorite Duck's recipe for a quick, easy and delicious dinner entree.

2 Tablespoons butter or margarine
2 center cut ham slices, 1/4-1/2 inch thick
1/2 cup applesauce
1/4 cup brown sugar
1 Tablespoon lemon juice

Melt the butter in a large skillet over low heat. Add the ham slices and fry for 3 to 5 minutes on each side. (If you use precooked ham, fry for only 2 minutes on each side.

While the ham is cooking, mix the applesauce, brown sugar and lemon juice in a small bowl. When the ham is ready, spread the applesauce topping on top.

Serves 4

SHIRLEY'S "CITY CHICKEN"

Actress Shirley Jones and her husband funnyman Marty Ingles are a winning combination both on the stage and in the kitchen, and so are two of their favorite recipes:

1 lb. each cubed beef, pork and veal
2 eggs
cracker meal
butter or margarine
herbs to taste
salt and pepper

Get 8 or 10 wooden skewers from your butcher. On each skewer, alternate cubes of beef, pork and veal until skewers are filled.

Dip entire skewer(s) into egg and cracker meal mixture till completely covered.

Brown skewers in pan (in butter or margarine) till brown on all sides.

Place in covered casserole with herbs of your preference. Salt and pepper and dot with butter.

Bake at 300 degrees for about 1 hour and 45 minutes. Baste a few times, uncover, and bake about 1/2 hr. more.

Serve with rice or buttered noodles.

MARTY'S NUTTY CHEESE ROLL

1 cup chopped walnuts.
1 8 oz. package of cream cheese
2 oz. Blue Cheese
4 oz. shredded sharp cheddar cheese
1/4 teaspoon of garlic powder
Dash of Worcestershire Sauce
1 Tablespoon brandy
1 Tablespoon Sherry wine.
Dash of white pepper

Blend all ingredients except walnuts.

Make into a ball and roll in chopped nut meats.

Cover with plastic wrap and refrigerate for two hours.

RICKY SKAGGS' CHICKEN PICKIN' CORN SOUP

Country great Ricky Skaggs doesn't spend all his time entertaining folks with his music. Once in a while, he cooks up a batch of his famous soup (a concoction that he invented) that makes his guests literally sing for their supper!

3 or 4 chicken breasts
4 medium potatoes
2 medium onions
1 can whole kernel corn
1 can cream style corn
1 can cream of chicken soup
1 can mushroom soup
5 Tablespoons Wesson oil
1 1/2 Tablespoons cornstarch
Salt and pepper to taste
McCormick's chicken seasoning

Cut the chicken into bite size pieces. Season with salt, pepper and chicken seasoning and brown in oil. Remove chicken from the pot. Combine soups with one can of water and bring to a boil. Add potatoes and onions. Add whole kernel and cream style corn. Bring to a boil and put chicken back in pot. Mix cornstarch with one cup water and add to soup, stirring well. Cover and simmer on medium heat for 45 minutes to 1 hour. Stir occasionally to prevent from sticking.

MAYOR ED KOCH'S PASTA WITH SUN DRIED TOMATOES

When past New York Mayor Ed Koch wandered the streets of New York, a familiar question he asked was "How am I doing?" Well, Mayor Koch, with this recipe, you are doing just fine!

1 medium onion, sliced.
4 sun dried tomatoes
1/4 cup dry white wine
3/4 cup cream
Fresh grated Parmesan cheese to taste
Salt and fresh ground black pepper to taste
1/4 lb. Capellini pasta

Saute onions in olive oil until transparent. Do not brown onions.
Add white wine, reduce by 2/3.
Add cream
Cook over high heat briefly
Add sun dried tomatoes and remove from heat
Add cooked pasta - return to heat
Add pepper and Parmesan cheese
Toss briefly and serve
Garnish with basil.

PHYLLIS DILLER'S ITALIAN SPAGHETTI

Phyllis Diller is a funny lady, except when it comes to cooking. Then, as the below recipe shows, she's about as serious as she can be!

1 1/2 pounds ground beef
3/4 cup Wesson oil
2 onions chopped coarse
One entire cluster of garlic cloves-- chopped fine
1 green pepper
Large can of tomatoes (#2 can)
1 small can tomato sauce
1 small can tomato paste
1 teaspoon of each: Marjoram, thyme, basil, poultry seasoning, garlic salt (not powder) onion salt (not powder) paprika, Lawry's seasoned salt.
1/2 teaspoon of each: Chili powder (not seasoning), cayenne pepper, dry mustard.
Menucci thin vermicelli #2 or Angesti Angel Hair or the finest spaghetti you can find.
Parmesan cheese
Garlic bread (serve with)

Brown the ground beef in 3/4 cup Wesson oil, chopping into bite size pieces as it browns, using large spoon or pancake turner. Cook together with chopped onions, garlic and green pepper.

After browning has eliminated all the red and you've done all sides, add the marjoram, thyme, basil, poultry seasoning, Italian seasoning, garlic salt, onion salt, paprika, Lawry's seasoned salt, chili powder, cayenne pepper and the dry mustard.

Pour in large can of tomatoes and cut bite size with a sharp knife and fork. Add small can of tomato sauce*. Add small can of tomato paste.*

Serve with the finest vermacelli you can find. To cook bring to fierce boil a pot of water to which you have added oil and salt. When done "al dente" (you have to taste), drain in colander and quickly run cold water through to keep from sticking together. Put back in pot and stir in 1/8 pound of butter.

Serve with grated parmesan cheese
Serve with garlic bread

*Rinse can with small amount of water and add to sauce.

DAVID L. WOLPER'S STUFFED GREEN PEPPERS WITH PASTA

Mega producer-director David L. Wolper, who produced the 1984 Los Angeles Olympic Games, the Washington D.C. bicentennial gala as well as TV blockbusters *Roots, Queen* and others gives us a taste of one of the gala events he produces in his kitchen.

1 Tablespoon extra virgin olive oil
1/2 onion, minced
1 small garlic clove, minced
1/3 cup small elbow macaroni
2 medium carrots, shredded coarsely
1 small zucchini, diced
1 cup salt-free chicken broth
1 teaspoon salt-free vegetable seasoning
1/2 teaspoon dried thyme, crushed
1 cup salt-free chicken broth
2 green or red sweet bell peppers, halved lengthwise and sliced
1/2 cup tomato sauce, heated
1 Tablespoon chopped parsley for garnish

Place oil in 2 quart, nonstick saucepan. Add onion, garlic and pasta. Saute for 2-3 minutes, or until golden in color, stirring frequently.

Add carrots, zucchini, chicken broth and seasonings. Heat to boiling, then reduce heat to a simmer and cover. Simmer for about 15 minutes, or until liquid is absorbed and pasta is tender.

Spoon hot pasta mixture into pepper shells and place in 10 inch skillet. Add broth and heat to

boiling. Lower heat to simmer, cover and simmer for 10 minutes.

Remove peppers to serving platter with slotted spoon. Drizzle with heated tomato sauce and sprinkle with parsley.

Serve as vegetarian meal with white rice on the side.

Makes for servings (1/2 stuffed pepper)

PHOTO BY EDDIE ADAMS / SYGMA

CLINT EASTWOOD'S SPAGHETTI WESTERN

This award winning recipe concocted by one of our favorite superstars may not be exactly what you expect for a spaghetti dinner . . . it's much, much better! Try it. It will definitely "make your day"!

3 Tablespoons vegetable oil
3 medium sized shallots, chopped, about 1/2 cup
1 medium-size rib celery, chopped, about 1/2 cup
1 small red bell pepper, cored, seeded and thinly sliced, about 1/2 cup
1 small yellow or green bell pepper, cored, seeded and thinly sliced, about 1/2 cup
2 large cloves of garlic, crushed
1 16-oz. can whole tomatoes
1/2 cup tomato puree
1/2 cup fish stock or bottled clam juice
1 bay leaf
1 teaspoon anchovy paste
1/2 teaspoon saffron threads or ground turmeric
Salt and freshly ground black pepper to taste
12 large mussels in shells, scrubbed and "beards" removed
1 ten oz. package frozen artichoke hearts, thawed and drained
4 large sea scallops, about 4 oz., quartered
1/2 cup heavy cream

2 Tablespoons Pernod liqueur, optional
half 16 oz. package spaghetti
1 6-1/2 oz. can of clams, drained and chopped
Celery leaves optional

In deep 12 inch skillet over medium heat, heat oil; add shallots, celery, red and yellow peppers and garlic. Cook about 10 minutes, stirring frequently until tender. Add tomatoes with their liquid, tomato puree, fish stock, bay leaf, anchovy paste, saffron, salt and pepper. Bring to a boil. Reduce heat to medium-low. Simmer, covered for 10 minutes. Meanwhile, in 3 quart saucepan, bring 1 inch water to a boil. Add mussels in their shells; cook, covered, 4 minutes just until shells open. Using sharp knife, cut mussels away from shells; reserve 12 half shells, discarding remainder. Rinse mussels under cold running water. Set aside. Add artichoke hearts, shrimp and scallops to skillet, increase heat to medium-high. Cook about 5 minutes, stirring frequently until shrimp turn just pink.Meanwhile, in deep four quart saucepan over high heat, bring 2 quarts water to a boil, 8 to 10 minutes. Stir in cream and Pernod if desired, into mixture in skillet; bring to boil. Reduce heat to low; simmer, covered 10 minutes. Meanwhile, add spaghetti to boiling water; cook 8 to 10 minutes until tender, stirring frequently. At end of cooking time, stir clams and mussels into mixture in skillet. Cook about 1 minute until heated through.

To serve: Drain spaghetti well; divide among 4 large, flat serving bowls. Remove shrimp, mussels and artichoke hearts from sauce; set aside, returning mussels to reserved shells. Spoon sauce over spaghetti; garnish each serving with one reserved shrimp, 3 mussels, 3 artichoke hearts, and celery leaves, if desired. Makes 4 servings.

DORIS DAY'S FETTUCINI PRIMAVERA

Perennial favorite Doris Day has come up with a quick, easy and delicious meal.

In hot butter and oil, stir fry 1/2 lb. sliced mushrooms and 2 julienned carrots. Add 1 cup chopped broccoli and 2 minced garlic cloves until softened. Add 1 1/2 cups cream, 1 tablespoon Dijon mustard and 1 lb. bay scallops. Simmer until slightly reduced. Now add 8 oz. cooked spinach fettucini, 2 slightly beaten egg yolks and 1/4 cup parmesan cheese. Toss until thoroughly combined. Serve at one on warmed plates. Garnish with more parmesan cheese and chopped parsley. Delicious!

Serves 2

JOHN RUSSELL

CHRIS EVERT'S SPAGHETTI

Athletes often stuff up on carbohydrates before a big game . . . Chris' spaghetti shows that she really knows how to cook both on and off the courts!

6 lbs. lean ground beef
4 medium large onions
7 Tbsp. olive oil
5 cloves of garlic, crushed
38 fluid ounces of tomato juice
23 large cans tomato paste
1 large can mushroom stems/pieces
2 Tbsp. oregano
2 bay leaves, halved
1 Tbsp. salt

Brown beef, onions and garlic in olive oil. Add remaining ingredients and simmer for one hour, stirring occasionally. Serve over freshly cooked spaghetti.

Serves 12.
Leftovers can be frozen.

ART LINKLETTER'S SPINACH NOODLE DISH

TV personality Art Linkletter could really throw a terrific House Party with the following recipe and have his dinner guests saying the darndest things about this easy, one dish meal.

1 cup grated cheddar cheese
1 lb. ground meat
6 oz. spinach noodles
1 5 oz. can tomato sauce
1 5 oz. can tomatoes
1 cup cottage cheese
1 cup sour cream
Garlic or garlic salt to taste
1 green pepper, mushrooms and sliced olives.

Fry meat, and drain off fat. Cook noodles. Simmer tomatoes, tomato sauce, garlic and green pepper, etc. about ten minutes. Put in casserole in layers, starting with noodles, then cottage cheese and sour cream, then meat. Top with grated cheese. Cook in oven at 350 until it bubbles.

Can be kept in refrigerator and reheated.

STP

RICHARD PETTY'S STUFFED GREEN PEPPERS

I'll bet Richard Petty in Car #43 "races" home when his wife, Lynda has this recipe on the dinner menu.

1 1/2 lbs. ground beef
1 medium onion, chopped fine
1 Tablespoon chili powder
2 eggs
1 cup catsup
1 cup cornflakes
Salt and pepper to taste
6 bell peppers, cut in half and cleaned

Boil peppers 5 minutes. Mix other ingredients together. Stuff peppers with the mixture and arrange in bottom of large ovenproof dish.

Sauce:

2 1/2 cups catsup & tomato paste (use more catsup than paste)
2 Tablespoons brown sugar
2 Tablespoons ground mustard
1 Tablespoon vinegar

Mix together, pour over peppers. Bake at 375 degrees for 30-40 minutes.

VANNA WHITE'S LAYERED PEA SALAD

TV personality Vanna White does a lot more than just turn letters on The Wheel of Fortune . . . she's also a whiz in the kitchen as is evidenced by the following delicious recipe. It's quick, easy, and get's an "A"!

In a 9x13x2" casserole dish, layer the following:

1 head chopped lettuce
1 cup diced celery
1/2 cup green peppers, diced
6 sliced hard boiled eggs
1 medium onion, diced
1 pkg. frozen peas, which have been thawed
8 to 10 cooked bacon strips, crumbled

Mix 2 cups Miracle Whip salad dressing with 2 Tablespoons sugar. Spread on top of layers in dish. Sprinkle one package of shredded cheddar cheese on top of that. Refrigerate until ready to serve.

TIM CONWAY'S CHICKORY & KIDNEY BEAN SALAD

Comedian Tim Conway has, I'm sure, been accused of being "full of beans" on at least one occasion during his career. This recipe proves that he really is . . . but in a delicious way!

2 heads of chickory
1 medium onion
1 can red kidney beans
3 Tablespoons olive oil
2 Tablespoons red wine vinegar
Salt and pepper to taste

Wash the chicory. Discard the tough outer leaves (unless you're an antelope). If you have a lettuce dryer, give the chickory a few spins in it.

Now pour the kidney beans and liquid into a bowl and mash lovingly with a potato masher.

Put the chickory into a bowl, pour the kidney beans on top. Then add the onion (sliced into small pieces), the olive oil, vinegar and salt and pepper. Toss until it looks suitable for serving.

I like this salad best with pita, Italian or French bread. It's yummy.

Once you get the hang of it, you can adjust the amount of onion, oil, vinegar, etc. to suit your own taste buds. ENJOY!

DALE EVANS' MEDITERRANEAN SALAD

It seems unlikely that Dale Evans came up with this recipe out on the range fighting the bad guys with husband Roy Rogers, but once she takes her spurs off, she's a whiz in the kitchen. This recipe will have anyone singing "Happy Trails to You . . ."

1 bunch romaine lettuce
1 bunch green onions
1 large clove of garlic, put through press
1 teaspoon salt
1/2 teaspoon coarse ground pepper
Juice of one lemon
Oregano leaves
Olive oil to cover top of torn romaine leaves

In wooden bowl, crush large cloves of garlic. Cream one teaspoon salt into the garlic, mixing thoroughly. Add juice of the lemon and cover with oregano leaves. Let stand for 30 minutes.

Chop green onions into 1/2" pieces and add to lemon juice mixture. Tear romaine over all. Sprinkle olive oil generously over the top and toss.

Serves 4

PAUL ANKA'S TABOULIE (MID-EASTERN PARSLEY SALAD)

Singer-songwriter Paul Anka says that there are many versions of this popular salad, but this variation is the one he grew up with.

3 bunches of parsley
2 medium-size ripe tomatoes
1/2 cup Bulgur (wheat germ)
4 green onions
Juice of 1 fresh lemon
2 Tablespoons olive oil
1 clove of garlic
Salt and pepper to taste

Wash parsley thoroughly, remove stems, finely chop and place in a large salad bowl. Dice tomatoes and add to parsley. Soak bulgur wheat in enough water to cover for 2 hours, then squeeze out water and add to parsley. Dice green onions, chop the garlic and add. Squeeze fresh lemon over the salad, sprinkle the olive oil over all, and salt and pepper to taste, and toss well. Serve with pita bread or Romaine lettuce.

Enjoy!!

WILLARD SCOTT'S SCOTCH EGGS

The TODAY Show's weatherman Willard Scott knows what he likes and for breakfast (or a midnight snack) the following recipe really fits the bill and makes the sun shine no matter what the weather is like outside.

3/4 lb. bulk pork sausage
1 egg beaten
12 hard cooked eggs
1/3 cup fine dry bread crumbs
Fat for deep frying

Divide sausage into 12 equal portions (1 oz. each). Shape portion into patty and wrap completely around 1 hard cooked egg, pressing edges together to seal. Dip sausage-wrapped eggs into beaten egg, then roll in bread crumbs until completely coated.

Cook eggs in preheated 375 degree deep fat until golden brown and heated through, 7 to 9 minutes. Drain on absorbent paper. Serve hot of cold. Yum!

JEANE DIXON'S COOL CUCUMBER YOGURT SOUP

Astrologer Jeane Dixon must have been star gazing really hard to have come up with such a heavenly soup for a warm summer day.

2 cups plain yogurt
1 cucumber pared and diced
3/4 teaspoon sea salt
Dash of cumin
1/8 teaspoon white pepper
1-2 Tablespoons honey
2 Tablespoons chopped walnuts or pecans*

Combine yogurt, cucumber, salt and pepper in electric blender. Whirl until pureed and blended. Add honey to taste. Add 2 tablespoons walnuts* and whirl briefly. Chill thoroughly. Sprinkle each serving with additional chopped walnuts.*

Note: One cup plain yogurt (made from partially skimmed milk) provides more than 1/4 of the U.S. recommended daily allowance of calcium. Particularly great for adults who find it difficult to drink their calcium in the form of milk.

HARRY LANGDON PHOTOGRAPHY©

GARY OWENS' CHILI STROGANOFF

Funnyman Gary Owens can't be put into any particular classification . . . Most folk remember him as the announcer with his hand up to his ear on Rowan and Martin's Laugh In, but Owens is the voice of hundreds of tv and radio commercials, has his own radio show in L.A., is acting in movies and is the voice of many of your favorite cartoon characters. In addition to his professional abilities, judging from the recipe below, he is also a top notch whiz in the kitchen!

2 pounds fillet of beef
*4 Tablespoons of butter**
1/2 Tablespoon of onion (chopped fine)
1 teaspoon chili powder
1/2 teaspoon cumin
*8 ounces sour cream***
8 ounces creme fraiche
Salt to taste
1/2 pound of mushrooms (sliced thin)

Place butter and onions in a pan and cook until onions are clear (low heat). Cut beef into long 1/2 inch by 1/2 inch strips, pound strips until they are one inch wide. Cook meat with onions until lightly brown (approximately 5 minutes). Set aside.

Deglaze pan with 3 tablespoons of water.

Add sour cream and creme fraiche, stir with wire whisk until smooth, use low heat . . . do not bring to a boil.

Add cumin, chili powder and salt.

Return reserved meat to cream mixture.

Add mushrooms . . . cover to keep warm until served.

Serve on bed of rice, noodles or kasha. Garnish with Chinese pea pods or mange tous peas (lightly blanched), chives and lemon wedges.

Serves 6

For lower cholesterol and/or calorie note the following:

*substitute 4 Tablespoons cooking oil.
**Substitute 8 ounces low fat yogurt.

Lady Bird Johnson

MRS. LYNDON B. JOHNSON'S STUFFED PEPPERS

Former First Lady, Lady Bird Johnson has a big family sitting around the table when they all gather for dinner. This quick, easy and delicious recipe will be a favorite around your dinner table as well.

Sear 1/3 cup chopped onion in small amount of oil in iron skillet for about 5 minutes. Add 2 pounds of ground meat and sear until done but not brown. Remove from heat and drain off all excess fat.

Return to heat, add 1/3 cup grated cheese, 1 teaspoon chopped fresh garlic and salt and pepper to taste.

Stir until cheese is melted. Remove from heat, add well-beaten egg.

Add 1/2 cup cooked rice to the mixture. Place meat mixture in peppers that have been seeded, washed and boiled in salted water for about 20 minutes.

Sprinkle dash of Ritz cracker crumbs on top. Bake for about 20 minutes in 400 degree oven.

BOB BARKER'S MEXICAN CHILI CON QUESO

It seems that Bob Barker, host of The Price Is Right wouldn't have any time at all to step into his kitchen to whip up a delicious meal, but he proves that theory wrong by contributing this tasty south of the border entre.

3/4 cup chopped onion
1/3 cup chopped green pepper
1 lb. Velveeta cheese
1 4 oz. can pimentos with liquid
1 Tablespoon chili powder
1 teaspoon garlic salt
Butter

Saute onion and green pepper in butter. Melt velveeta cheese and mix with onion and green pepper. Add can of pimentos with liquid. Season with chili powder and garlic salt.

Serve with tortilla chips.

BARBARA BUSH'S MEXICAN MOUND

Former First Lady Barbara Bush has a huge family to feed when they all get together, and the recipe below really satisfies their taste buds. As she puts it, "This recipe is easy to make, loved by all who love Mexican food. The ingredients are easy to keep in the house. Children or guests can all help with the chopping or grating. It's fun! "

A-1 package of corn chips
B-2 lbs. ground beef
C-1 package Taco Seasoning mix
D-1 cup grated yellow cheese
E-1 or 2 small chopped onions (not minced)
F-10 chopped ripe black olives
G-1 chopped tomato
H-1 cup sour cream
I-Lettuce (a cup shredded)
J-1 medium can of frozen avocado dip

Follow instructions on Taco Seasoning mix for browning meat. I serve this meal in my kitchen, a big pot of meat simmering on the stove, a wooden salad bowl of corn chips and seven bowls (D through I) of the remaining ingredients around the table. Start with a mound of corn chips, a spoon of piping hot meat, cheese, etc.

REBA McENTIRE'S HOT 'N' SPICY CHUNKY BEEF CHILI

Country music's sensation Reba McEntire can really belt out a song, and proves that the can really whip up a terrific meal.

Preparation time: 20 minutes
Cooking time: 2 hours and 10 minutes

2 1/4 lbs. lean boneless beef chuck, cut into 3/4" pieces
1 cup coarsely chopped onion
2 cloves garlic, minced
2 Tablespoons vegetable oil
1 teaspoon salt
1 can (28 oz.) plum tomatoes, broken up!
1 cup water
1 can (6 oz.) tomato paste
3 Tablespoons chili powder
1 teaspoon dried oregano leaves
1/2 teaspoon crushed red pepper pods
1 cup chopped green bell pepper
6 Tablespoons each shredded cheddar cheese and sliced green onions.

Brown beef (Half at a time) with onion and garlic in oil in large frying pan or dutch oven. Pour off drippings. Sprinkle salt over beef. Add tomatoes, water, tomato paste, chili powder, oregano and crushed red pepper. Cover tightly and simmer 1 1/2 hours until beef is tender. Add green pepper and continue cooking , uncovered for 30 minutes. Sprinkle each serving with cheese and green onion slices.

Makes 8 servings of 1 1/2 cup each.

***333 calories, 36 g protein, 16 g fat, 13 g carbohydrate, 5.7 mg. iron, 731 mg. sodium, and 102 mh. cholesterol.

Enjoy!

TERRY BRADSHAW'S FAVORITE

Pittsburgh Steeler's ex-quarterback Terry Bradshaw could sure tear them up on the football field, but he can really bring the opposition to their knees at mealtime with his favorite recipe.

1 can lima beans, navy beans or butter beans
1 can pork n' beans
1/2 lb. bacon
3/4 lb. hamburger
1 medium onion, cut fine
1/2 cup celery

Sauce:

1 Tablespoon Worchestershire sauce
1/2 cup brown sugar
1 Tablespoon prepared mustard
1 Tablespoon vinegar
1/2 cup catsup

Cut bacon into small pieces and fry. Pour off fat. Add hamburger and cook until meat loses it's color (do not brown.) Drain and add onions, celery and all the beans. Pour into a casserole dish. Heat sauce and mix well. Bake in a 350 degree oven for one hour.

LISA WHELCHEL'S HOMEMADE CHOCOLATE SQUARES

Although Lisa's character Blair on the hit TV series "FACTS OF LIFE" was not a terribly compassionate and friendly sort, her recipe for chocolate squares proves that Lisa really is as sweet as sugar.

1/3 cup evaporated milk plus
1/2 cup evaporated milk
14 oz. square type caramels
3/4 cup margarine
1 package German Chocolate cake mix
1 cup chopped nuts
6 oz. chocolate chips

Melt caramels and mix with 1/3 cup of the evaporated milk. Set aside. Melt together and set aside 3/4 cup margarine and 1/2 cup evaporated milk. Mix 1 package of the german chocolate cake mix with 1 cup of chopped nuts; add in margarine mixture. Take half of this mixture and press in bottom of 9x13" pan. Bake for 8 minutes at 350 degrees Fahrenheit.

Remove and sprinkle the 6 oz. of chocolate chips on hot crust, then drizzle on the melted caramel mixture. Press on remaining dough. Bake for 18 minutes at 350 degrees. Cool slightly, then refrigerate for 1 hour. Cut into 24 squares.

Have a happy week and keep smiling!

ROY CLARK'S SUNBURST LEMON BARS

It has been said that country singer Roy Clark is a real sweetie, and his recipe for Sunburst Lemon Bars aptly proves that point.

Crust:

2 cups flour
1/2 cup powdered sugar
1 cup margarine/butter, softened

Filling:

4 eggs, slightly beaten
2 cups sugar
1/4 cup flour
1 teaspoon baking powder
1/4 cup lemon juice

Glaze:

1 cup powdered sugar
2-3 Tablespoons lemon juice

Heat oven to 350. In large bowl, combine 2 cups flour, 1/2 cup powdered sugar and margarine at low speed until crumbly. Press mixture evenly into bottom of ungreased 9x13" pan. Bake for 20-30 minutes or until light brown.

In large bowl, combine eggs, sugar, 1/4 cup flour and baking powder; blend well. Stir in lemon juice. Pour mixture over warm crust. Return to oven and bake 25-30 minutes or until top is light brown. Cool completely.

In small bowl, combine powdered sugar and enough lemon juice for desired glaze consistency; blend until smooth. Drizzle over cooled bars. Cut into bars. Makes approximately 36 bars.

NANCY REAGAN'S VIENNA CHOCOLATE BARS

Former first Lady Nancy Reagan spent much of her husband's term in office entertaining dignitaries at state dinners at the White House. I'm sure this tasty dessert appeared on the banquet tables quite often.

2 sticks of butter
1 1/2 cups sugar
2 1/2 cups flour
1/4 teaspoon salt
1 cup chocolate bits
2 egg yolks
1-10 oz. jar of your favorite jelly
4 egg whites
2 cups finely chopped nuts

Cream the butter and 1/2 cup sugar. Add the flour and knead with fingers. Pat out on a greased cookie sheet and top with butter.

Bake for 15 to 20 minutes at 350 degrees until lightly browned. Remove from oven, spread with jelly and top with chocolate bits.

Beat egg whites until stiff. Fold in remaining sugar and nuts.

Gently spread on top of jelly and chocolate.

Bake for about 25 minutes at 350 degrees. Cut into squares or bars

KENNY KINGSTON
FAMED INTERNATIONAL PSYCHIC

PSYCHIC KENNY KINGSTON'S "SWEET SPIRIT ANGEL DELIGHT"

Psychic to the stars Kenny Kingston can tell a person more about themselves than they might want to know . . . and with an incredible accuracy rate, he's one of the leading psychics in the world today. But, this man of incredible talents also can add delicious desserts to his list of achievements. This one is terrific.

For crust:

1 cup flour
1 Tablespoon sugar
1/2 cup margarine

Mix well, as you would for a pie crust. Press mixture in the bottom (only) of a 9x9 inch baking dish. Bake at 350 degrees for 15-20 minutes.

Then, heat one can of Diamond A rhubarb. While rhubarb is heating, mix together:

3 Tablespoons flour
1/2 cup sugar
2 egg yolks
1/2 cup milk

Beat until smooth. Add to hot rhubarb and cook until thick. Cool, then pour into the baked pie crust.

For topping, mix:

2 egg whites
1/2 cup sugar
1/4 teaspoon cream of tartar

Cover rhubarb mixture with this meringue topping and bake at 300 degrees until brown on top. When done, cut into squares. Serve slightly warm or cool.

This recipe is liked even by those "sweet spirits" who aren't rhubarb lovers! Try it. It's attractive, too!

BARBARA CARTLAND'S CAMFIELD CHOCOLATE CAKE

Famed romance novelist Barbara Cartland has a "simply delicious" chocolate cake recipe that is sure to win the hearts of any hero or heroine.

3 Tablespoons cocoa powder
2 Tablespoons caster sugar
3 Tablespoons water
150 ml. / 1/4 pint milk
1 teaspoon vanilla essence
100 g. /4 oz. butter
225 g. /8 oz. brown sugar
3 eggs, separated
175 g. /6 oz. plain flour
Pinch of salt
2 teaspoon baking powder
25 g. /1 oz. cornflour

Filling

175 g. /6 oz. unsweetened chocolate
(preferably raw sugar chocolate)
50 g. /2 oz. butter
150 ml. / 1/4 pint cream
450 g. /1 lb. icing sugar

Place cocoa, caster sugar and water in the top of a double boiler and melt slowly, stirring until thick and smooth, then add the mild and vanilla extract, mix well and set aside to cool.

Cream the butter and sugar and beat in the egg yolks and the chocolate mixture. Then sift together

Barbara Cartland

the flour, salt, baking powder and cornflour and fold into the cake mixture. Whip the egg whites until they are stiff and fold them into the mixture. Grease three 7 inch cake pans, line them with greased ovenproof paper and pour the mixture evenly into them. Bake in a moderate oven, 160-180c (325-350 degrees), gas 3-4 for 30 minutes. Turn out on a wire rack to cool.

To make the filling, melt the chocolate with the butter and cream over hot water until smooth. Sift the icing sugar into a large bowl and mix in the chocolate cream. Spread between layers of the cake and over the top and sides.

Serves 8

JACKLYN ZEMAN'S PINEAPPLE SOUR CREAM CAKE

General Hospital's favorite R.N. can give a shot with the best of them, but she really takes her best shot in the kitchen with this terrific dessert!

1-8 oz. can crushed pineapple in juice
1/2 teaspoon baking soda
1 package (2 layer) yellow cake mix
1 package (4 servings) vanilla, pineapple cream or pistachio Jello instant pudding mix
4 eggs
1 cup (1/2 pint) sour cream
1/4 cup of oil

Combine pineapple with juice and soda into mixing well. Combine cake mix and remaining ingredients in a large bowl. Add pineapple mixture. Blend, then beat at medium speed for 4 minutes. Pour into greased and floured 10 inch fluted tube or tube pan. Bake at 350 degrees for 50-55 minutes. (Cake will pull away from side of pan. Do not UNDERBAKE.) Cool in pan for 15 minutes. Remove from pan and finish cooling on rack.

SALLY STRUTHERS' PORTLAND PEACH PIE

"Not too many people think of peaches when they think of Portland . . . it's usually apples that get the press! But we had two huge peach trees in our back yard and every year, I couldn't wait for the peaches to ripen so I could help my mother (Mother Struthers) make her famous peach pies and I would take bags of peaches to all the neighbors on the block."

2 cups milk
2 eggs
1/2 cup sugar
3 Tablespoons cornstarch
1/2 teaspoon of vanilla
4-6 peaches (depending on size of pie) cut into thick slices
Graham cracker crust
Whipped cream

In medium saucepan, mix milk and eggs with beater. Combine sugar, cornstarch and salt in a bowl. Slowly pour the dry mixture into the egg mixture and stir with a wooden spoon. Cook over medium heat, stirring constantly, until mixture boils and thickens. Take off heat, add vanilla and a pat of butter. Stir and let cool. Slice peaches just before use and arrange in pie crust. Pour cooled mixture over peaches. Cover with whipped cream and store in refrigerator until set.

DUDLEY MOORE'S "72 MARKET STREET KEY LIME PIE"

We all know Dudley Moore as an accomplished actor and musician, but he is also a restaurateur. He is co-owner of 72 Market Street in Venice, California. Here, Mr. Moore shares one of his establishment's favorite desserts.

Crust:

3 oz. graham crumbs
1 oz. all purpose flour
1 oz. sugar
2 oz. melted butter

Filling:

1 can sweetened condensed milk
6 egg yolks
3 oz. persian lime juice
3 oz. key lime juice

DIRECTIONS:

Pat crust into 9" pie pan. Bake 15 minutes at 250 degrees. Cool. Combine all filling ingredients. Do not overmix. Pour into crust and let set at room temperature for 8 hours. Then refrigerate before serving.

HELEN GURLEY BROWN'S SKINNY CHOCOLATE MOUSSE

As the editor of one of the nation's leading magazines, Cosmopolitan, Helen Gurley Brown knows a lot about what's in fashion and what is not. Since it's always fashionable to look good, she offers this delicious (and lo calorie!) dessert .

1 envelope chocolate D-Zerta
2 cups skim milk
2 teaspoons vanilla
2 Tablespoons Hershey's chocolate syrup
1 oz. brandy
2 packages Sweet 'n' Low or Equal

Mix the milk and chocolate, add other ingredients. Cook, stirring constantly, until pudding begins to thicken. Pour into bowls and chill. This makes two big portions of about 200 calories each or four small ones at 100 calories each.

SALLY JESSY RAPHAEL'S STRAWBERRY FROZEN YOGURT PIE

Talk show host Sally Jessy Raphael has discussed almost every subject imaginable on her show . . . except maybe cooking. This is one of her favorite recipes . . . and you'll be amazed how something so delicious can be so quick and easy!

8 oz. strawberry yoogurt
1 small container sour cream
1/2 cup chopped fresh strawberries
1 prepared graham cracker pie crust

Blend yogurt, sour cream and strawberries together. Pour into pie crust and freeze until solid.

Serves 6

Note: Substitute strawberry yogurt and fruit for your own favorites. Use lowfat yogurt and sour cream if you are counting calories.

JOAN VAN ARK'S FRESH FRUIT PIZZA

Knot's Landing's Joan Van Ark likes to keep herself looking good. Part of her regimen is a healthy diet. This delicious dessert makes eating fresh fruit a gratifying experience.

2 eight oz. packages of softened cream cheese
1/2 cup margerine
1 1/4 cups flour
1/4 teaspoon salt
1/3 cup sugar
1 Tablespoon lemon juice
1 cup whipping cream
Fresh fruit (strawberries, blueberries, kiwi)
Apricot preserves
1 Tablespoon water

Combine 1/2 package cream cheese and margerine. Mix well until blended.

Add flour and salt. Mix and form into a ball. Chill.

On lightly floured surface, roll into 14" circle. Prick with fork. Bake at 425 degrees for twelve to fifteen minutes.

Combine remaining cream cheese, sugar, lemon juice. Fold in whipped cream. Spoon onto crust. Cover with fresh fruit. Brush with preserves thinned with water and heated in a microwave oven.

Chill and serve.

RICHARD STOLTZMAN'S LINZER TORTE

"The aroma of cinamon, cloves, almonds and cocoa mixed with the raspberries will turn your kitchen into a Viennese pastry shop. Just add a little Mozart . . . I love being on the stage and performing clarinet literature for audiences. This linzer torte is also a classic and will definitely put you on center stage . . . with lots of bravos! Desserts, after all, get the most applause"

1 cup flour
2 Tbsp. cocoa
1/2 tsp. cinnamon
1/4 tsp. ground cloves
1/2 lb. salted butter, softened
1/2 cup plus 1 Tbsp. sugar
2 egg yolks
2 cups ground almonds
1 cup raspberry preserves
1 egg white
1 Tbsp. water
Confectioner's sugar

Mix the flour, cocoa, cinnamon and cloves together in a bowl and set aside.

Cream the butter, and beat in the half cup of sugar. Beat in the egg yolks. Gradually blend in the almonds and the flour mixture to make a thick batter.

Using about half the batter, spread an even

layer, one eighth to 1/4 inch thick on the bottom of an 8 or 9 inch round baking pan with removable bottom. Spread the jam over the batter to within 1/2 inch of the edge, taking care not to break the layer of batter.

Spoon the remaining batter into a pastry bag fitted with a large tube, 1/2 inch in diameter. pipe 3 to 5 parallel lines of batter straight across the layer of jam from one edge to the another. Give the pan a quarter turn and pipe 3 to 5 more parallel lines across the pastry from edge to edge. Pipe the remaining batter around the edge. Any excess batter can be used to form round cookies on a baking sheet. Fill with jam and bake.

Refrigerate for one hour. Preheat the oven to 300 degrees.

Beat the egg white with the remaining sugar and the water until frothy. Brush this mixture over the pastry strips and bake for one hour. Allow to cool completely.

Before serving, sift Confectioner's sugar over the top. Remove the sides of the pan and serve.

Serves 8
Total preparation time: 3 hours.

RANDY TRAVIS' OLD-FASHIONED OATMEAL COOKIES

Country singer Randy Travis has won more Grammys and Country Music Awards than you can shake a stick at; but my guess is that we would be a strong contender for first prize if he entered the Pillsbury Bake-Off with the following recipe.

1 cup of raisins
1 cup of water
3/4 cup shortening
1 1/2 cups sugar
2 eggs
1 teaspoon vanilla
2 1/2 cups Gold Medal Flour
1 teaspoon baking soda
1 teaspoon salt
1 teaspoon cinnamon
1/2 teaspoon baking powder
1/2 teaspoon cloves
2 cups oats
1/2 cup chopped nuts

Simmer raisins and water over medium heat until raisins are plump, about 15 minutes. Drain raisins, reserving the liquid. Add enough water to reserved liquid to measure 1/2 cup. Heat oven to 400 degrees.

Mix thoroughly the shortening, sugar, eggs and vanilla. Stir in reserved liquid. Blend in remaining ingredients. Drop dough by rounded teaspoonfuls

Photo Credit: John Paschal

about 2 inches apart on ungreased baking sheet. Bake for 8 to 10 minutes or until light brown.

If using self-rising flour, omit soda, salt and baking powder.

Makes about 6 1/2 dozen cookies.

ROSE MARIE'S CHICKEN A LA ROSE MARIE

Everybody knows Rose Marie as the wisecracking sidekick to Morey Amsterdam on the old Dick Van Dyke Show. She's wise, all right! Just try this entree at dinner sometime.

8 chicken breasts
Garlic to taste
Progresso flavored bread crumbs
Pinch of oregano
1/2 cup water
1/2 cup lemon juice
1 teaspoon parsley flakes
Salt and pepper to taste
1 cup olive oil

Wash chicken, skin and fillet. Cover chicken thoroughly with bread crumbs. Place pieces in a baking dish. Chop garlic very fine over and around the chicken. Sprinkle on salt, pepper and oregano. Mix water, lemon juice and parsley flakes together, pour half over chicken. Pour olive oil over chicken. Bake at 350 degrees about one hour.

Pour the rest of the lemon juice mixture over the chicken and serve hot.

ANA-ALICIA'S CHINESE CHICKEN SALAD

Falcon Crest's favorite vixen proves that she can cook, too!

1/2 lb. boiled chicken, shredded and soaked in soy sauce for a few hours.
2 oz. rice sticks fried for a few seconds in hot oil
4 finely sliced green onions
2 Tablespoons sliced almonds
2 Tablespoons toasted sesame seeds
1 head of shredded lettuce

Combine dressing ingredients separately and then toss with salad ingredients.

Dressing

1 cup salad oil
1 Tablespoon sesame oil (this adds a lot of flavor)
3 Tablespoons vinegar
1 teaspoon salt
1/4 teaspoon pepper
2 teaspoons sugar

Shake well until all ingredients are well mixed.

ISABEL SANFORD

WEEZY'S BOSTON CHICKEN

Anyone who is a fan of "The Jeffersons" knows that Isabel Sanford, who played Louise on the show, had a maid to whip up the meals. In real life, Sanford is quite adept in the kitchen, as the following recipe proves.

Serves: 4

8 pieces of chicken
4 large whole potatoes
1 cup Thousand Island or Russian salad dressing
1 cup apricot-pineapple preserves
1 package instant onion soup mix
1/4 cup grated onion
1 dash of cinnamon

Wash chicken pieces and potatoes and set aside. Preheat oven to 300.

In a mixing bowl, combine the salad dressing, preserves, onion soup mix, grated onion and cinnamon into a past-like substance.

Spread the pieces of chicken in a single layer in a shallow baking dish or pan, the bottom of which should be lightly covered with cooking oil.

Take the uncooked potatoes and slice them into halves, the long way, and place them along the sides of the pan, so that you have a tight fit of chicken pieces and potatoes filling the pan.

"Paint" with a brush or knife the sauce mixture to completely cover the chicken and potatoes. Cover with aluminum foil and bake for 40 minutes. Then, remove the foil and bake at 375 for 15 minutes more, or until chicken and potatoes have a golden brown glaze.

This dish can be served as is or complemented with a green vegetable and/or small salad.

DAVE BRUBECK'S RATATOUILLE

Jazz great Dave Brubeck can sure keep a joint jumpin' with his incredible music. On the home front, his wife, Iola, knows how to keep things jumpin' at the dinner table when she whips up this delicious and easy to prepare vegetarian dish.

2 medium sized eggplants
6 tomatoes (preferably Italian pear shaped)
1 cup white cooking wine
Mozzarella cheese
1 clove of garlic
Cheddar and parmesan cheese
Bread crumbs
Italian herbs
Black pepper
Olive oil

Saute onion and garlic in oil. Saute zucchini and eggplant separately and let drain on a paper towel. Sprinkle Italian seasoning and pepper over cut up vegetables. Chop up mozzarella and cheddar, and stir in with vegetables and cut up tomatoes.

Top with sliced tomatoes and sprinkle with parmesan. Add bread crumbs. Pour white wine over the mixture. Bake 25 minutes in 350 oven, covered . . . just long enough for the juices to simmer. Each piece of vegetable should remain firm.

Serve with brown rice and a summer salad.

JOAN FONTAINE'S CHICKEN FONTAINE

Academy award winner Joan Fontaine is probably best known for her roles in Rebecca and Jane Eyre. She won an Oscar for her role in Suspicion, and wrote "No Bed of Roses", her autobiography. This delicious recipe also shows that when it comes to cooking, she is a true professional.

4 chicken breasts
4 Tablespoons flour
4 Tablespoons butter
Juice and grated rind of one lemon
1/4 cup dry white wine (or sherry)
2 Tablespoons capers
Salt and pepper

Lightly pound chicken breasts. Place in bag containing flour, salt and pepper. Shake until coated, then remove from bag and shake of excess flour.

Heat skillet with butter until butter reaches bubbling point. Saute breasts for 2 minutes on each side. Add the juice and rind of lemon. Add dry white wine or sherry and the capers. Cover and cook for 1 minute, then serve.

OLIVIA DE HAVILLAND'S SPINACH SALAD

Movie legend Olivia De Havilland's portrayal of Melanie in the epic classic "Gone With The Wind" is probably her best remember role, but you will remember her with great fondness every time you serve her delicious spinach salad.

Ingredients: To a suitable amount of raw, freshly washed spinach leaves, add one can or drained grapefruit sections, which have been cut in half, and six ounces of cashew nuts. Pour over this combination a dressing made of:

1/3 cup vinegar
1 cup sunflower oil
1 Tablespoon celery seed
1/4 grated onion
1/3 cup sugar
1 teaspoon salt
1 tsp dried mustard.

Combine ingredients and shake well.

PAT SAJAK'S CARMELIZED ONION COD

Game show host Pat Sajak claims that this is his favorite recipe.

3 large onions
2 Tablespoons olive oil
2 Tablespoons (1/4 stick) butter
1/4 teaspoon ground turmeric
1 1/4 teaspoons ground ginger
1 lb. cod (2 1 1/2 inch thick steaks)
Salt and black pepper

In a very heavy skillet, saute the onions, turmeric, and ginger over low heat in the oil and butter until carmel colored, about 30-40 minutes. Season the cod with the salt and pepper and let sit while the onions are cooking.

Put a layer of the onions in the baking dish, put the cod on top and cover with another layer of onions. Cover the dish with a tight lid of aluminum foil, sealing the edges. Bake at 400 degrees for 8 to 12 minutes.

Serve with Yogurt soup and steamed baby carrots.

BUFFALO BOB SMITH'S BARBECUED RIBS

There's probably not a person alive today that doesn't know Buffalo Bob Smith and remember him and Howdy Doody with great fondness. Well, apparently Buffalo Bob didn't spend all his time in Doodyville clowning around with Clarabelle and the gang. Here's one man who really knows how to barbecue!

Enough ribs to feed a hungry group (Canadian baby back ribs are the best)

Glaze:

1/2 cups apricot preserves
1/2 cup mayonnaise
1/2 cup Catsup
1/4 cup soy sauce
1 teaspoon ground ginger
1 teaspoon garlic powder
1 teaspoon minced onion

Mix above ingredients together.

Preheat grill. Cut lean spare ribs into 3 or 4 rib sections, about 1 1/4 lb. per serving. Turn grill to low and keep top pen throughout. Place ribs on grids–cook 18-20 minutes until golden brown. Turn ribs and cook other side another 18-20 minutes. Remove from grill. Make heavy duty foil pan and place on grill. Put ribs in pan, cover with glaze and turn ribs to coat other side with glaze. Repeat every five minutes until done (approximately 20 minutes).

Chicken pieces and pork chops are also delicious done this way.

Invite me over anytime!

Buffalo Bob Smith

FRANK BORMAN'S CHICKEN FRUIT SALAD

Astronaut Frank Borman didn't have his head in the clouds when he came up with this delicious salad for a warm summer day.

2 cups cooked chunked chicken
2 cups cooked macaroni
1 cup chunked cantaloupe
1/4 cup chopped celery
3/4 cup seedless grapes
1/4 cup slivered almonds
1/4 cup raisins

Dressing:

1/2 cup mayonnaise
1 teaspoon cider vinegar
1 Tablespoon honey or sugar

Add dressing to all ingredients and mix well. Serve on a bed of lettuce and garnish with strawberries

Yours Cruelly
Elvira

ELVIRA'S BEDEVILED EGGS

Elvira, Mistress of the Dark, had this commentary about the following recipe. "Eggs have always played an important part in sorcery. What was it that Merlin showed King Arthur how to pull out of the stone? Right. The magic sword . . . Eggscaliber."

"What did the golden goose lay? I said what . . . not whom. Okay. Right the second time. Eggs."

"Who was Shakespeare's greatest tragic hero? Of course. Omelet."

"And how about Al Bumin, who runs the delicatessen on Fairfax but dabbles in the black art of mixing egg cream sodas in the back room?"

"The point is that eggs and the occult have a lot in common. Which is why I always serve bedeviled eggs at all of my pagan rituals. "

"How do you bedevil an egg? One way is to put it through an IRS audit. But here's an easier recipe . . . "

6 eggs
1 teaspoon vinegar
1/8 teaspoon salt
Dash worcestershire sauce

1/16 teaspoon horseradish, grated
1/4 cup mayonnaise
1 teaspoon french mustard
Dash pepper
Sliced olives stuffed with pimentos.

Bring eggs to boil slowly in a copper pot (to prevent green tinge to yolks.) Boil eggs for 15 minutes and cool for 10 minutes. Remove shells and cut in half lengthwise. Remove yolks with a spoon. Combine seasonings with yolks and mash together. Then, refill whites with yolk mixture.

Garnish with olive slices and serve.

LEROY NEIMAN'S OYSTERS MOSCA

Most folks probably think all renowned artist LeRoy Neiman's only talent is art. His illustrations for Playboy Magazine and ABC sports are legendary. But leave him alone in the kitchen, and he can really whip up culinary masterpieces as well.

2 cups Progresso Bread crumbs
1 Tablespoon crushed red pepper
2 lemons juiced
3/4 cup olive oil
1 clove of garlic
3 Tablespoons chopped parsley
Salt to taste
1 quart oysters, drained

Combine all ingredients, except oysters. Place oysters in a baking dish, ramekins or shells. Top with mixture.

Bake a 350 degrees until oysters curl and then place under the broiler until slightly browned.

A great hors d'oeuvre or main dish!

STEPHEN KING'S BASIC BREAD

Maven of the macabre, Stephen King, can conjure up all sorts of horrible situations in the text of a novel, but when it comes to baking bread, he creates an entirely different atmosphere. "Baking bread is one of the ways I relax. I like kneading it, and I love the smell of it, the way it fills the house and makes your mouth water."

2 packages of dry yeast dissolved in 3/4 cup of warm (not hot)
water, with sugar as directed on the package
2 cups lukewarm milk
3 Tablespoons sugar
1 Tablespoon salt
3 Tablespoons shortening
8 cups of flour, all purpose of bread flour
Melted butter

Dissolve yeast. Add milk, sugar, shortening, and half the flour, mix until smooth. Mix in rest of flour until dough is easy to handle. Knead on floured surface until smooth--10 minutes should do it. Put in a greased bowl, cover with dish towel and let it rise about an hour, until double. Divide dough in half, shape into loaves, place in greased loaf pans, brush with butter and let rise another hour. Bake at 425 about 25-30 minutes, until brown. To test for doneness, tap to see if they sound hollow. Brush with butter if you like.

Yield: 2 loaves

DICK GREGORY'S AVOCADO DRESSING

One of the foremost comedians of the 60's, Dick Gregory is also an activist for racial equality and healthy living. His famous diet has helped many overweight people overcome their obesity. The following recipe proves that healthy food can also be delicious!

1 ripe avocado
Juice of one lemon or orange
*Honey to taste**
*Grated onion to taste**

Mash the pulp of one avocado. Add the juice of 1 orange or 1 lemon very gradually to season. Whip with a rotary beater until the consistency of whipped cream.

*Add a little honey to the mixture if used on a fruit salad, or some finely grated onion if used on a vegetable salad.

AUDREY MEADOWS' NOODLES WITH CHICKEN AND PEANUT SAUCE

It's doubtful that Alice Kramden ever fixed a delicious meal such as this one for Ralph, but Audrey Meadows sure knows how to please her man when she is not in front of the camera!

8 oz. (dry) spaghetti or other thin noodles (about 4 1/2 cups cooked)
4 teaspoons cornstarch
1 1/2 cups water
2 Tablespoons peanut butter
2 Tablespoons soy sauce
2 Tablespoons cider vinegar
2 Tablespoons sugar
2 teaspoons ground coriander
2 Tablespoons grated fresh ginger root
6 scallions, slivered
1 Tablespoon vegetable oil
12 oz. boneless, skinless chicken, cut into bite-sized chunks
4 cups bean sprouts

Boil pasta in 3 quarts water until tender but firm. Meanwhile, dissolve cornstarch in 2 tablespoons water, add peanut butter and stir until smooth. Then add the remaining water, soy sauce, vinegar, sugar, coriander, ginger root and 4 slivered scallions. Mix well. In wok or heavy skillet, heat oil. Stir fry chicken pieces over high heat for five minutes. Remove with slotted spoon and set aside.

Reheat the residual oil in the pan and stir fry

bean sprouts for 2 minutes. Return chicken to pan, and add sauce, and heat for about another minute, stirring until sauce thickens. Toss drained pasta with chicken. Garnish with remaining 2 slivered scallions.

Serve with sliced oranges and steamed broccoli topped with sesame seeds.

Serves 4.

MARIO ANDRETTI'S GNOCCHI

If you like Italian food (and who doesn't), race car driver Mario Andretti has contributed a recipe sure to make a paisan out of all of us. It may blow a diet or two, but after you taste it, you won't care!

4 lbs. Idaho potatoes
4 cups flour
2 eggs, beaten
1 stick butter
2 Tablespoons salt

Add salt to potatoes and boil with jackets on. Peel and mash potatoes while hot. Place butter in center of hot mashed potatoes. When butter has melted (about 15 minutes), mix potatoes thoroughly. Cover with dish towel and allow to cool. Make a small well in the center of the potatoes and pour eggs in and mix well. Gradually add flour and additional salt to taste. Knead well to form dough. Separate mixture into four equal parts. Sprinkle each with flour. Roll each portion into a roll the thickness of a sausage. Slice in pieces slightly thicker than a half inch. Gently roll each piece on flat grater, slightly curling each piece. Pieces should resemble macaroni shells. Cook in 4 quarts of boiling salted water about 20 to 30 seconds. (Cook about 1/3 of the total amount at one time.) Gnocchi will rise to the top of boiling water when done. Gently scoop out with slotted spoon as they rise to the top.

Prepare brown sauce ahead of time. Sprinkle parmesan cheese on top of cooked gnocchi and top with generous amounts of sauce.

Sauce:

2 lbs. beef, cut in cubes
1 large onion, chopped
1-8 oz. can Hunt's tomato sauce
1 box Spatini gravy (powder form)
1 teaspoon Accent
Salt and pepper to taste
2 Tablespoons fresh herbs, finely chopped together--parsley, thyme, marjoram,
and 4 cloves of garlic.
3 Tablespoons butter

Brown onion in a pot with butter. After browned, pour water, a few drops at a time over onions. Use approximately 1/4 cup of water. Add herbs and stir for a few minutes over medium heat.

Season the meat with seasoned salt, seasoned pepper and Accent. Then place the meat in a pot. Slowly fry the meat until the water disappears. (This is a very important step.)

In a medium-size bowl, stir the Spatini gravy powder into the tomato sauce. Then, slowly add 2 cups of water and mix thoroughly. Gradually add this mixture to the beef cubes. Immediately turn the burner down and simmer. Don't let it stick to the bottom. Then add more water for the thickness you want. Let the sauce simmer for an hour and a half or until the meat is tender.

Serve over gnocchi or pasta.

SHERMAN HEMSLEY'S SPICY CHICKEN MEAT LOAF

One could never imagine George Jefferson going into the kitchen and whipping up dinner. But that was way back when. Sherman Hemsley proves that sometimes food can be so good it's like a religious experience. AMEN to that!

4 medium carrots
2 onions
1 bell pepper
2/3 cup wild rice, washed and drained
2 lbs. ground chicken
1 1/4 Tablespoons salt
1/2 teaspoon pepper
1 egg
1 Tablespoon mustard (optional)

Barbecue sauce:

3/4 cup ketchup
2 Tablespoons Worcestershire sauce
1 Tablespoon lemon juice
2 Tablespoons honey
1/2 teaspoon hot chili powder
1/2 cup water

Chop carrots, onions and bell pepper into small pieces. In a large mixing bowl, combine vegetables with the ground chicken, rice, salt, pepper, egg and mustard, if desired.

Place mixture into a 2 1/2 lb. meat loaf tin. Bake at 350 degrees for 1 1/4 to 1 1/2 hours.

Meanwhile, make sauce by combining all ingredients in a saucepan. Bring to a boil and simmer until liquid is reduced by about one third.

Serve sauce hot with meat loaf.

Preparation time: 10 minutes
Cooking time: 1 1/4-1 1/2 hours
Serves 6

DOUGLAS FAIRBANKS JR.'S CHICKEN CASSEROLE

Legendary screen idol Douglas Fairbanks, Jr. has been living the good life lately. As this recipe demonstrates, eating well is the best revenge!

White bread, crusts removed, soaked in milk
Cooked chicken, cut in pieces (preferably breasts)
Onion, chopped or cut into rings
Ham (preferably smoked) sliced
Half and half (or milk or cream)
Butter
Salt and pepper to taste

Preheat oven to 350 degrees. Line a pyrex-type casserole dish with bread. Lay in alternate layers of cooked chicken pieces, a little onion, a slice of ham, another layer or milk-soaked bread, more chicken and ham, and so forth until dish is full.

Add half and half or milk, or full cream if you want it richer; dot with butter; salt and pepper to taste, and bake in oven until thoroughly heated through. If you want the top crusty, heat under broiler for a few seconds.

This can be made ahead, refrigerated and then heated later.

GEORGE GOBEL'S CHILI RELLANO CASSEROLE

The late "Lonesome George" couldn't possibly have been lonesome if he whiped up this "muy savroso" Mexican dish and let a few friends know about it.

1 lb. hamburger
1 large onion
2 7 oz. cans Ortega peppers
1 small can tomato sauce
12 oz. grated cheese
Taco seasoning
1 egg
1/2 cup milk
1 1/2 Tablespoon flour
Salt and Pepper

Brown meat and onions. drain. Add tomato sauce and seasonings. Simmer.

Mix topping: 1 egg, milk, flour, and a dash of salt and pepper.

Layer two (2) layers of meat, onion, cheese mix, with chilies. Pour on topping and bake at 350 degrees for 45-50 minutes.

Cool five minutes before serving.

JOE MONTANA'S VEAL PICCATA

San Francisco Forty Niner Joe Montana scores a touchdown with this recipe! It would make a delicious dinner for a small group of your favorite people.

1 lb. veal scallops, pounded thin
Flour
Salt
Freshly ground pepper
3 Tablespoons olive oil
1 clove garlic, minced
1/2 cup dry white wine
1/2 cup chicken broth
3 Tablespoons capers
1 small lemon, peeled with all white removed, seeded and diced
2 Tablespoons butter
2 Tablespoons fresh parsley, chopped

Flour veal, season with salt and pepper. Saute in oil until slightly browned, about 2-3 minutes. Remove from pan and keep warm. Add garlic to oil and saute briefly.

Add wine and chicken stock and bring to a boil. Reduce to 1/3 cup. Stir in capers and lemon and return to a boil. Swirl in butter and parsley and continue cooking until sauce thickens and turns creamy.

Dip veal slices into sauce to coat. Arrange on a platter and spoon the remaining sauce over the scallops.

A suggested wine to accompany veal: Pinot Noir or Cabernet Sauvignon.

Serves 4

PHOTO BY: CAROL L. NEWSOM

MARTINA NAVRATILOVA'S DUCK AND DUMPLINGS

Tennis champion Martina Navratilova has won just about every trophy imaginable for her excellence in tennis. The following recipe should win her yet another trophy for excellence in the kitchen.

1 duck, 5-6 lbs.
Salt
Carraway seeds
1/2 pint chicken stock

Dumplings:

1 lb. flour
8 fluid oz. milk
4 fluid oz. water
5 large slices bread, cut in quarters
4 egg yolks
1/2 tsp. baking powder
1/2 tsp. salt

Sprinkle duck with salt and carraway seeds. Stand on rack in baking pan and cook in oven preheated to 375 degrees, allowing 20 minutes per lb. weight. Pour over chicken stock as necessary. Halfway through cooking time, pour off grease and turn duck. Meanwhile, prepare dumplings.

Put milk, water, egg yolks, baking powder and salt in a bowl and mix well. Add flour and mix well again. Finally, add bread and work to a doughy consistency. Divide into four portions. In a large pan, boil salted water. When boiling, add dumplings and cook for 25 to 30 minutes. Take care not to let the dumplings stick to the bottom of the pan.

Serve with duck and sauerkraut.

DAN BLACKBURN'S CHERRIED PHEASANT

Ex-Washington correspondent and award winning journalist Dan Blackburn is usually so busy out on the road covering the news for CNN (he was also with NBC for 12 years and CBS for another 4), writing books (a best seller on cross country skiing) or following the President around the country that one would think he'd be eating out every night . . . but, this multi talented personality also loves to cook. Here is one of his favorite pheasant recipes:

1 pheasant
Freshly ground salt and pepper
1 can of black cherries
1/3 cup Kirsch cherry liqueur
3 or 4 apples, quartered
2-3 Tablespoons of butter

Rub the pheasant inside and out with salt and pepper. Then thoroughly rub the skin with Kirsch. Melt butter and add the remaining Kirsch to the melted butter. Keep warm. Baste the entire bird with the Kirsch and butter mixture. Stuff the bird with the apples.

Place the basted and stuffed bird in a preheated 400 degree oven. Immediately reduce the heat control to 350 degrees. Cook for one hour. Meanwhile, combine liquid from black cherries with the remaining Kirsch and melted butter mixture. Add enough black cherry liquid to match the amount of remaining butter and Kirsch. Every 15 minutes, baste the bird with this mixture. Test for doneness. Do not overcook. Remove the bird from the oven to a warm plate. Remove the apples from the cavity. Lightly drizzle remaining black cherry juice over the bird and add the black cherries to each individual serving.

Eat and enjoy. Serves 2-3 people.

ERMA BOMBECK'S TACO SALAD

Erma Bombeck is a humorous author, syndicated columnist, housewife and mother. If you don't know who she is, you've been doing your cooking on another planet. With her busy schedule, it seems doubtful that she has any time to cook but her contribution to the book proves that she is one woman who has time to "do it all!"

1 head of lettuce, finely chopped
1/2 lb. ground sirloin of beef
2 large tomatoes, diced
1 1/2 cups grated cheddar cheese
3/4 cup (Own favorite dressing)
3 Tablespoons of sour cream

Wash and chop the lettuce in advance. Place lettuce in a colander so that all moisture can drip out of the lettuce before preparing the salad. Place colander in the refrigerator. Crumble the sirloin and cook over medium heat till just done.

Put the chopped lettuce, diced tomatoes, cooked warm sirloin and 3/4 cup of the grated cheese in a large mixing bowl. Add your favorite dressing and toss well. Divide the salad on 6 plates. Sprinkle remaining 3/4 cup of grated cheddar cheese evenly on top of each serving. Put 1 1/2 teaspoons sour cream on top of each salad. I like this served with Toasted Tortilla Triangles. Makes 6 servings.

BOB HOPE'S FAVORITE MINT SAUCE

Being on the road so much, it's hard to imagine Bob Hope being able to sit down and enjoy a quiet meal at home. When he does get the chance, here is one of his favorite things to serve with roasted lamb.

1 bunch of fresh mint
3/4 cup white wine vinegar
1/4 cup lemon juice
1/4 cup water
1/2 cup of honey
1/2 Tablespoon salt
Dash of Worcestershire sauce
1/2 Glass green mint jelly

Cut or chop mint very fine and combine with other ingredients. Let steep for several hours.

Serve with roasted lamb.

JULIE ANDREWS' SOUP FRANCINE

The hills will surely come alive on a cold night when you make this savory soup for your family and friends. The best part is, you can use your favorite vegetables.

Melt a large tablespoon of clarified butter (or margarine or corn oil) in a wide pan.

Add:

1 diced onion
1 diced medium potato
Vegetables of your choice, cut up in small pieces (if you use a stalk vegetable, dice the stalk and all)
Ground pepper
Seasonings of your choice
(Parsley Patch all purpose is very good . . . sometimes a little curry powder helps, also.)

Leave all the ingredients in the melted butter on low heat and simmer until onions are soft and a light golden colour. Stir frequently. It takes about 15 minutes.

Then add stock, chicken or vegetable, a chicken cube with added boiling water, for example. Bring to a boil, then let simmer for another 15 minutes.

Let cool. Blend in blender, and if too thick, add a little more stock , or if soup needs more zest, add V-8 Juice. As it is stored in the fridge, it may thicken, so add more V-8 as the week goes by.

Note: Amount of stock used is optional. Julie cooks for a large family, so she uses about a quart. But for single people or a couple, a pint should do.

Also, if cooking for more people, use 2 potatoes, and more vegetables, etc.

Carrot soup and broccoli soup turn out just marvelously, but cauliflower, peas, tomatoes, celery, watercress, etc. can be used equally as well. And leftover vegetable soup is good too!

BENNY HILL'S SALAD NICOISE

English funnyman Benny Hill made us laugh for a long, long time, but there is nothing funny about his favorite salad. It will tickle your tastebuds!

1 twelve and one half oz. can water packed tuna, drained
2 Tablespoons lemon juice
1 Tablespoon of capers
1/4 teaspoon of salt
1/4 teaspoon of pepper
3/4 lb. fresh baby green peas
1 lb. small red potatoes, unpeeled
3/4 lb. cherry tomatoes, halved
1 medium sized sweet yellow pepper, seeded and cut into julienne strips
1/2 medium sized purple onion, thinly sliced
Vinaigrette (recipe to follow)
1 large head curly leaf lettuce, torn
1/4 cup Nicoise olives
2 Tablespoons chopped fresh parsley

Combine tuna, lemon juice, capers, salt and pepper. Toss gently and set aside. Wash beans, trim ends and remove strings. Cook beans in a small amount of boiling water for five minutes or until crisp/tender. Drain. Plunge beans into ice water to cool. Drain and set aside. Boil potatoes for 15 minutes, drain. Cool. Cut potatoes into fourths. Place beans, potatoes, tomatoes, pepper strips and onions into separate bowls. Add 2 tablespoons

vinaigrette into each bowl. Toss gently, cover and chill.

Arrange lettuce on a large serving platter, mound tuna mixture in center of platter, and arrange the chilled vegetables around the tuna. Add remaining dressing to salad. Sprinkle with olives and parsley.

Serves 6

Vinaigrette Dressing

1/2 teaspoon chicken bouillon granules
1/2 cup boiling water
2 Tablespoons red wine vinegar
1 Tablespoon lemon juice
2 cloves minced garlic
1 Tablespoon vegetable oil
1/4 teaspoon dried whole oregano

Dissolve bouillon granules in boiling water. Set aside and let cool. Combine remaining ingredients. Blend well with wire wisk.

WARE
OF
CATS

TIPPI HEDREN'S SPINACH DIP

Actress Tippi Hedren starred in two of Alfred Hitchcock's greatest movies "The Birds" and "Marnie." These days, she's devoted to caring for some 67 exotic cats (of the lion and tiger variety) at her Shambala Preserve in Southern California. Although she's more concerned with feeding her wild animals, Tippi still has the occasional opportunity to feed some of her friends with delicious dishes such as the following appetizer. According to Tippi, "If you love garlic, you'll love this!!!"

8 oz. sour cream
1 cup mayonnaise
1/2 tsp. lemon juice
1 tsp. Italian dressing
6 chopped green onions
1 pkg. chopped spinach (frozen)
6 chopped arlic cloves
1 Tbsp. chopped parsley
1 round loaf of bread

Mix first 8 ingredients together in a bowl and let the flavors mingle for several hours, then place the dip in the hollowed-out loaf of bread for serving.

Use pieces of bread as a carrier for this taste delight!

Recipe idea is from Restaurant Nana Rosa in Beverly Hills.

BETTY WHITE'S CHICKEN WINGS PACIFICA

While Betty White's Emmy Award winning alter ego Rose Nyland on "The Golden Girls" might have called this recipe *Chicken Wings St. Olaf* (and used herring as the main ingredient!) we prefer the original recipe.

3 lbs. chicken wings or drumettes
(or more--they disappear fast)
1 stick butter or margarine
1 cup soy sauce
1 cup brown sugar
3/4 cup water
1/2 tsp. dry mustard

Arrange wings in shallow baking pan. Heat butter (or margarine), soy sauce, sugar, water and mustard until butter and sugar melt. Cool. Pour over wings and marinate at least two hours, turning once or twice.

Bake in the same pan at 375° for 1 ¼ to 1 ½ hours, turning occasionally. Drain on paper towels.

TOOL TIME

RICHARD KARN'S SHRIMP SALAD

On ABC's hit series "Home Improvement," actor Richard Karn plays a master carpenter. In his personal life, he seems to be a master in the kitchen as this recipe will surely prove.

1 head savoy cabbage
1 1/2 Tbsp. mayonnaise, or to taste
Green onions to taste
A pinch of sugar
Juice of 1/2 a lemon
Pepper to taste
1 lb. medium shirmp

Chop the cabbage and green onions. Mix all remaining ingredients together. Chill and serve.

This can be used as a side dish or as a main course, depending on the amount made. Richard always makes this salad as an accompaniment to the Karn family's traditional Thanksgiving dinner.

NANCY LOPEZ-KNIGHT'S ENCHILADA CASSEROLE

On the golf course, no one can surpass her. In the food department, Nancy Lopez-Knight really scores a hole in one for this delicious main course.

1 lb. ground beef
1 Tbsp. butter
3 cans (10 oz.) cream of chicken soup
1 1/2 (soup) cans of milk
3 small cans green chilis, chopped
10-12 flour tortillas
1/2 cup Longhorn cheese, grated
2-4 Tbsp. choppen onion

In medium-size fry pan, cook ground beef with 1 Tbsp. butter until well browned. Drain and set aside. In a large saucepan, combine the coup, milk and chilis; cook over medium heat until mixture is well blended and smooth. Remove from heat and set aside.

Wrap the tortillas in foil and place in a 300 degree oven to just warm through. Remove from oven. Lay each tortilla flat. Place 3 Tbsp. of meat in center, and sprinkle with grated cheese and onion. Roll up and place in a lightly buttered 9"x13" baking dish. Continue with balance of tortillas until dish is full. Pour soup mixture over all. Sauce should surround and completely cover the enchiladas. Sprinkle additional grated cheese on top. Bake, covered, for 30 minutes at 350 degrees.

Note: 1 1/2 cups cooked and diced chicken may be substituted for the ground beef.

RICHARD SIMMONS' YENTL LENTIL SALAD

Health and fitness guru Richard Simmons has devoted his life to helping people get fit and stay healthy. The following recipe is one of the many of Richard's delicious recipes which prove that being on a diet doesn't mean you can't have good tasting food and diet, too!

2 cups cooked lentils
1 1/2 cups peeled, seeded, chopped tomatoes
1 cup chopped parsley
1/2 cup diced celery
1/2 cup chopped green pepper
1/2 cup chopped red onion
1/4 cup chopped mint
1/4 cup lemon juice
1 Tbsp. olive oil
1 tsp. salt
1/4 tsp. pepper
1/8 tsp. each garlic powder and cumin
Lettuce leaves
Mint leaves (optional)

In large mixing bowl, combine all ingredients, except lettuce and mint leaves, mixing thoroughly. Chill Serve on bed of lettuce. Garnish with mint leaves if desired.

Makes 3 servings.

Michael Lamont Photography

FRED TRAVALENA'S SPAGHETTI AND MEATBALLS

Onstage, Fred Travalena takes on the persona of some of the most celebrated persons in the world; but in the kitchen, he becomes "Spaghetti Master."

Sauce:

2 28 oz. cans of whole peeled tomatoes
1 6 oz. can of tomato paste
1 cup water
1 big chopped onion
3 big chopped garlic cloves
2 Tbsp. olive oil

Blend first three ingredients in a blender

Cover bottom of fry pan with oil; saute onion and garlic.

Combine all of the above ingredients in a large pot.

Add:

4 bay leaves
1/2 cup grated fresh romano cheese
2 Tbsp. sugar
1 large beef or pork bone
Parsley flakes or fresh parsley to taste

Cook for approximately 1 ½ hours.

Remove bone and bay leaves before serving

Meatballs:

2 Lbs. chopped ground round beef
4 eggs
3/4 cup chopped onions
4 chopped garlic cloves
Salt and pepper to taste
4 slices chopped bread
1 Tbsp. milk
1/2 cup grated romano cheese

Mix all ingredients
Make meatballs and fry in olive oil
Drop in sauce the last half hour of cooking

BUDDY HACKETT'S CHINESE CHILI

Funnyman Buddy Hackett is not someone you'd expect to see in the kitchen preparing dinner for friends. You expect to see him up on stage, making people laugh. Well, at first glance, this recipe can cause a titter or two by virtue of it's name alone, but once you give it a try, you'll realize that this is no laughing matter. It's delicious!

2 lbs. chili meat with 5% suet (can use ground chuck)
1 Tablespoon chili powder
2 Tablespoons Farmer's Ground California dry chili
1 large onion, diced
1 pinch of oregano
1/2 teaspoon granulated garlic
1 teaspoon salt
3 cups diagonally sliced celery
1 cup sliced onion
1 cup sliced water chestnuts
1 cup sliced bamboo shoots
1 cup bean sprouts
1 No. 5 can beef consomme
1/2 teaspoon salt

Saute the meat along with the diced onion, chili powder, ground dry chili, oregano, garlic and 1 teaspoon salt. When well cooked, add enough flour to take up the fat. Simmer for 20 minutes. Add the can of beef consomme to chili and simmer for 2 hours, stirring frequently.

In separate saucepan, saute the celery and sliced onions in a small amount of vegetable oil. Keep stirring so that the vegetables will cook fast and evenly. When crisp, add the remaining vegetables and salt; cook for five minutes. While still hot, drain all liquid from the vegetables. Add the chili to the vegetables and you will have Buddy Hackett's personal creation of Chinese Chili.

DOLLY PARTON'S CORN PONE

"Pones," cornmeal cakes shaped like ovals, originated with the Algonquin Indians, and are quite common in the South. Other parts of the country would love them as much, if they would give them a try. With this recipe from Dollywood, Dolly Parton's theme park in the Smokey Mountains of Tennessee, everyone nationwide can learn to love corn pone as a delicious switch from bread or dinner rolls. The best part is that they are easy to make!

2 cups cornmeal
1 teaspoon salt
2 teaspoons all purpose flour
2 teaspoons bacon grease
Milk (use enough to make a stiff batter) about 1 cup

Mix all ingredients together, then form pones by hand and put on a greased baking sheet. Bake 12 to 15 minutes at 425 degrees.

Makes about 1 1/2 dozen, depending on size.

DAVID HOROWITZ'S SHRIMP A LA DAVID

It's hard to imagine consumer advocate David Horowitz coming home from a hard day of "fighting back" and preparing an elaborate meal, but apparently he's quite a good cook, because he can eyeball a recipe and know just how much of what to put in. As most cooks know, the hardest part of writing a recipe is trying to figure out how much of this or that we use . Here is Shrimp a la David, minus the amounts of ingredients necessary. I suppose they depend on how many people you're cooking for. Good luck!

Large size tiger shrimp
Prosciutto ham
Imported Swiss cheese
Sweet butter
Fresh garlic cloves
Fresh made Italian seasoned bread crumbs
Beaten egg
Cooking sherry
Fresh chopped parsley
Paprika
Small diameter unsliced bread

Preheat oven to 325 degrees. Chop garlic into melted butter. Fillet shrimp, dip in beaten egg and then in bread crumbs. Add cooking sherry to melted garlic butter. Saute shrimp in butter until brown. Prepare thinly sliced garlic bread. Layer shrimp, prosciutto ham and Swiss cheese on garlic bread. Bake until cheese is melted. Serve hot, garnished with chopped parsley and paprika.

GOVERNOR GEORGE DEUKMEJIAN'S APPLE MUFFINS

California Governor George Deukmejian's wife, Gloria, chose these recipes as a couple of the Deukmejian family favorites.

1/2 cup apple juice
2 teaspoons baking powder
1/3 cup sugar
1/2 teaspoon cinnamon
1/4 teaspoon salt
1 cup chopped apples
1/4 cup oil

*Topping:
1 egg
1 1/2 cups all purpose flour

Combine apple juice, sugar, oil and egg. Blend well. In a separate bowl, combine flour, baking powder, cinnamon and salt. Add liquid to dry ingredients, stirring until just blended. Fold in apples. Divide batter among 10 lightly greased muffin cups. Sprinkle with topping. Bake in 350 degree oven for 20 minutes or until toothpick inserted in center comes out clean.

*Topping:

Combine 1/3 cup finely chopped walnuts, 2 tablespoons of packed brown sugar and 1 teaspoon cinnamon.

COOPER HUCKABEE'S CRAWFISH ETOUFFEE

Being born and raised in the South is a blessing in itself, but having a mother who is practically a gourmet cook makes actor Cooper Huckabee twice blessed. He shares his mother's delicious recipe for crawfish etouffee, which, by the way can be made with shrimp instead.

1/4 pound butter
2 large onions chopped
1 bell pepper chopped
2 stalks celery chopped
2 cloves of garlic minced
Salt, freshly ground black pepper and red pepper (cayenne) to taste
Tabasco sauce to taste
2 lbs. peeled crawfish tails
4 Tablespoons flour
1-2 cups water
4 chicken bouillon cubes
Green onion tops, chopped

Melt butter in large, heavy skillet. Saute vegetables in butter for 30 minutes. Add seasonings to taste; then add crawfish tails. Saute for a minute and then stir in flour. Continue sauteing for about 3 minutes; then add water, chicken bouillon and green onion tops. Simmer 10 to 15 minutes. Sprinkle with parsley if desired. Serve over cooked rice.

Serves 4-6

DR. JOYCE BROTHERS' MEAT LOAF

Famed "Doctor of the Mind" Dr. Joyce Brothers has no problem solving the problems that affect us in our daily lives. Now she shows us how to solve the problem of a terrific dinner that the entire family will love.

2 cups fresh bread crumbs
3/4 cup minced onion
1/4 cup minced green pepper
2 eggs
2 lbs. ground chuck
2 Tablespoons horseradish
2 1/2 teaspoons salt
1 teaspoon dry mustard
1/4 cup regular or evaporated milk
3/4 cup Catsup

When it's convenient, prepare bread crumbs, minced onion and green pepper.

About 1 hour before serving, start heating oven to 400 degrees.

In a large bowl, with fork, beat eggs slightly. Lightly mix in chuck, then crumbs, onion, and pepper. (Meat will be juicier and more tender if you handle it as little as possible.) Add horseradish, salt, mustard, milk, 1/4 cup catsup and combine lightly but well.

In a bowl, shape meat into oval loaf. Transfer to shallow baking dish or broil-and-serve platter. Smooth into shapely loaf. Spread top with 1/2 cup catsup. Bake for 50 minutes.

Serve from baking dish or broil-and-serve platter, pouring off excess juices. Or, with two broad spatulas, lift loaf out of baking dish onto heated platter. Spoon some of the juices over the meat. (Nice chilled, then served sliced, too!)

Makes 8 servings.

P.S. If you prefer a soft, moist exterior, bake meat loaf as directed in a 9"x5"x3" loaf pan. Pour juices from pan after baking. Unmold meatloaf onto cake rack, then place, right side up, on heated platter. Use juices for making gravy if desired.

SAMMY CAHN'S HAWAIIAN CHICKEN BAR-B-Q

The late Academy Award-winning songwriter Sammy Cahn knew as much about a scrumptious Bar-B-Que as he did songwriting. Follow his instructions carefully, and you'll have such a mouthwatering fare that you definitely won't be able to keep the neighbors at bey!

Fill a blender one third full of peanut oil
Add one half cup of dark brown sugar
Add four or five cloves of garlic
Add fresh ground black pepper (to taste)
Add one fourth cup of soy sauce
Add one fourth cup of white vinegar
Add pure honey to sweeten (to taste)

(Note: Keep repeating the above mixture until you have enough sauce to immerse the amount of chicken you want to marinate. The chicken should be quartered and marinated for at least six hours! (Or more--the longer the margination, the better the result!) The chicken should also be turned every so often to insure complete margination. It should be kept in a cool place while marinating.)

To insure perfect results, it is terribly important that the fire be a slow fire. Because of the ingredients, the chicken will seem to blacken and burn. And this can be controlled so it is a golden color if the fire is not too hot and burns low and slow! It takes between three quarters of an hour to an hour for the chicken to cook through if the fire is right (and it better be!) Therefore, allow enough time for the fire to burn down before placing the first batch (bone side down) on the fire. If you faithfully follow the above you and your guests should sit down to a meal which is sheer ambrosia!!!

The final touch and the bit that is showmanly and magic is the spray of a fine white sauterne wine which is applied just as the chicken is served. This is best applied with the use of a spray bottle, and just enough to cover the chicken with a fine mist.

To conclude, watch the fire, follow the above and enjoy!!

Sammy Kahn
(From ancient Jewaiian recipe)

CAPTAIN KANGAROO'S (BOB KEESHAN'S) COUNTRY CHICKEN LOAF

All the years we were growing up with Captain Kangaroo, we all wondered just what it was that the Captain had in those large pockets of his and why Mr. Green Jeans hung around so often. It might have been his Country Chicken Loaf!

2 cups diced cooked chicken
1/2 cup chopped cooked carrots
1 cup cooked peas
1/2 cup chopped celery
1 Tablespoon minced green pepper
1 cup bread crumbs
1/2 cup milk
2 egg yolks, beaten
1 teaspoon onion juice
1/2 teaspoon thyme
1 teaspoon lemon juice
1/4 teaspoon curry powder
1 teaspoon salt
1/4 teaspoon pepper

Force chicken, carrots and peas through a food chopper. Add remaining ingredients, mix well and place in a greased loaf pan or ring mold. Bake in moderate oven (350 degrees) until firm, about 40 minutes. Serve with cream or mushroom sauce.

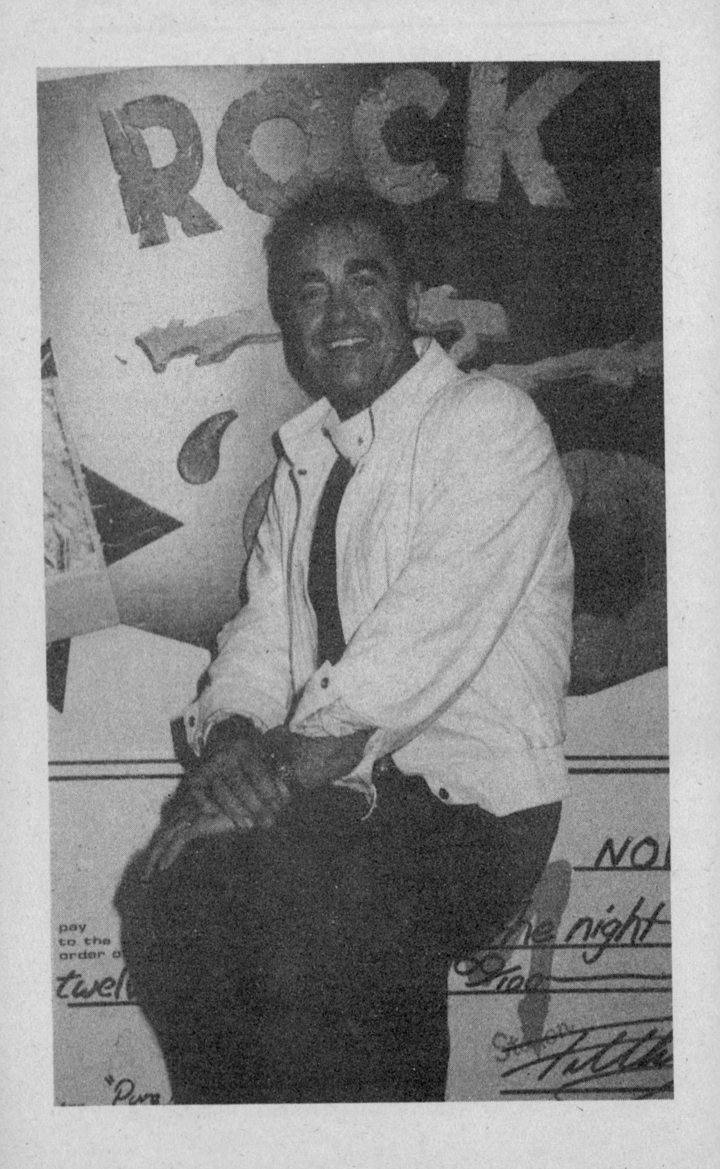
ROCK
pay
to the

FILTHY McNASTY'S ROULADEN AND RED CABBAGE

Entertainer and Los Angeles legend Filthy McNasty is also the owner of L.A.'s "FM Station Live", one of the West Coast's leading nightclubs. Filthy's mother, Gertrud, was a terrific cook and in her memory, he wants to share one of her best recipes.

Rouladen:

3-4 lbs. top round. (Cut into 10 very thin slices pounded out into rectangular shapes, about 3"x5".)
2 cups finely chopped onion
2 cups finely chopped raw bacon
10 teaspoons mustard
Salt and pepper to taste.

Gravy:

16 oz. sour cream
3/4 cup buttermilk
1 beef bouillon cube
1/4 cup flour
1/8 cup cornstarch
2 Tbsp. butter

Take sliced beef rectangles and lay out separately on counter. Evenly spread about one teaspoon mustard on each piece of meat, then spread equal amounts of chopped onion and uncooked chopped bacon in a thin layer on top of each slice of meat. Salt and pepper meat to taste.

Tightly roll each piece of stuffed meat into a fat cigar shape and secure with toothpick. Brown meat in butter over medium heat on all sides in frying pan. When meat is brown, transfer (along with pan drippings) to casserole dish and bake in 350 degree oven about 40 minutes. At the end of cooking time, remove meat from dish and set aside. Place pan drippings in frying pan.

To make gravy, add the sour cream, buttermilk, bouillon cube, flour and cornstarch to pan drippings. Mix well and simmer (stirring frequently) until heated through and thick. To serve, place meat on serving platter and pour gravy on top.

Red Cabbage:

2 heads of red cabbage, shredded
1/2 - 3/4 cup sugar
1 Tbsp. salt
1 tsp. black pepper
20 whole cloves
1 or 2 apples, finely chopped
1 onion finely chopped (optional)
1/2 cup vinegar
1 cup water
1 cup lard

Blanch red cabbage in boiling water until soft but still on the crispy side. Add vinegar and simmer over low flame for 10-15 minutes. Add remaining ingredients and simmer for another 15 minutes until cabbage is soft, but not mushy. Stir often. When done, add lard and mix through over low heat.

Serve cabbage and rouladen together with boiled potatoes.

This is a great make ahead dish. Actually, it tastes better the second day.

DR. RUTH'S SASSY FRUIT SALAD

Famed sex therapist, Dr. Ruth Westheimer har been teaching us how to have better relationships with our loved ones for years. To paraphrase an old cliché, "the way to your mate's heart is really through his/her stomach. Serve this wonderfully delicious fruit salad and watch your mate beg for more!

It is best to prepare one day in advance.
We can mix up the order of these ingredients:

2 grapefruits
2 oranges
1 apple
2 pears
2 bananas
2 persimmons, if available
2 kiwi fruit, if available
5 dates
1 cup sliced strawberries
2 Tbsp. raisins
1/2 cup chopped or shredded coconut
2 Tbsp. frozen orange and apple juice concentrate
1/3 cup Curacao or fruit liqueur
1/4 cup sweet red wine
chopped almonds or walnuts (according to taste)

Cut up the oranges and grapefruits in a large bowl. Squeeze out the juice and discard the membranes.

Cut up the rest of the fruit and mix with coconut, raisins, juice, liqueur and wine. Refrigerate overnight.

TO SERVE: place in individual fruit bowls , or glasses, and sprinkle with almonds or walnuts. Can be also served in a large bowl as part of your buffet.

Optional: If you want to go all out, top each serving with ice cream or whipped cream, or dress with a combination of 1 cup sour cream and 3 tablespoons of maple syrup.

LILLIE LANGTRY'S SHRIMP CANTONESE

The Lillie Langtry is a wonderful restaurant located inside the Golden Nugget Hotel and casino in downtown Las Vegas, Nevada. Chef Su Pong makes this terrific dish that it is worth a whole trip to Vegas just to try it!

8 medium raw shrimp,
peeled and cut in halves
1 oz. chopped pork
1/2 tsp. ground salted black bean
1/4 Tsp. fresh chopped garlic
1/8 cup dices, peeled water chestnuts
2 whole green onions, cut in 2" strips
1 whole egg (raw)
1 Tbsp. cornstarch
1/8 cup vegetable oil
1/4 Tsp. salt
1/4 Tsp. sugar
1/4 Tsp. sesame oil

Heat oil, garlic and black bean. Place shrimp and water chestnuts in hot oil also. Stir 3/4 cup of unsalted broth. Let simmer. Add corn starch and whole egg. Mix well. Garnish with ggreen onions and serve.

Happy Dinning.

WINK MARTINDALE'S PASTA PRIMAVERA

Veteran radio and television personality Wink Martindale proves that he must not only be living right, but is eating right as well!

1 lb. pasta (Angel Hair or green spinach noodles)
1 lb. plum tomatoes OR 3 lbs. canned fresh Italian tomatoes, drained.
1 lb. broccoli florettes
1 lb. zucchini
6 fresh mushrooms
1 large chopped onion
6 shallots, peeled
4 carrots, chopped
1/2 cup chopped fresh Italian parsley leaves
4 small garlic cloves, crushed and peeled
2 Tbsp. minced fresh basil leaves or 1 Tbsp. dried
1 Tbsp. Italian seasoning
1/4 cup freshly grated Parmesan cheese
4 Tbsp. olive oil

Fill a large pot with cold water. Bring water to a boil. Add salt, if desired. Then add the pasta and cook, stirring occasionally and cook to taste. Drain pasta and return to pot.

While pasta is cooking, wash and trim the vegatables.

Pour oil into a skillet and add all chopped vegetables, garlic and seasoning. Cook for 10-15 minutes.

Now pour the sauce over the pasta and add Parmesan cheese. Add salt and pepper to taste, and serve.

With a salad, this sould serve 8-10 people.

Marvelous Marvin Hagler

Although the marvelous one doesn't find a lot of time to spend in the kitchen, but he wrote in to say that his favorite food is lobster. In fact, one day he ate seven of them! He also loves baked fish, spaghetti and meatballs, and soul food. Most of the time, he goes out to eat.

King Juan Carlos of Spain

As one might expect, the ruler of a nation seldom finds time to pop down into the kitchen of the royal palace and fix a feast for forty or so of his closest friends, but King Juan Carlos favorite foods are meat, fish and salads. He suggests visiting a restaurant that specializes in Spanish food for a real taste of Spain.

George Burns

Legendary nonogenarian George Burns has had a cook for many years. He claims to like everything she prepares for him, but did offer this little bit of inside information: "If the soup is stove hot and there is a bottle of Catsup on the table, you'll find one very happy George Burns."

Charlton Heston

Charlton Heston writes: "Thanks for asking me to be a part of the cookbook you're assembling, but I don't cook and will thus not be contributing a recipe. I hope you will accept instead my best wishes for the success of your book and good luck."

"WE'RE REALLY VERY SORRY, BUT . . ."

A LETTER from Buckingham Palace sends it's regrets with the following explanation from one of Queen Elizabeth's Ladys-in-Waiting: "I am commanded by the Queen to write and thank you for your letter, but because of Her Majesty's rules in these matters, I regret it is not possible for her to do as you ask. When I tell you of the many requests that The Queen receives, I feel sure you will understand the reason for these rules and that it would be most unfair to make any exception to them."

FROM THE Palace of Monaco: "Her Serene Highness Princess Caroline of Monaco has asked me to reply to your recent letter, for which she thanks you. I regret that due to the large numbers of similar requests received daily by Her Serene Highness, She regrets that She is unable to answer your appeal."

STEVIE WONDER: "Stevie does not cook and will be unable, therefore, to assist you."

SENATOR JOHN GLENN: "Thank you for your letter requesting a recipe for your Celebrity Cookbook. I regret that Senator Glenn has a policy of providing recipes only for non-profit or charitable causes."

JULIA CHILD: "I am sorry to say I just cannot contribute a recipe to your cookbook. As you might imagine, we get an enormous number of requests like yours and being a one woman operation, I simply cannot fill them for the following reasons: All my recipes that we do on TV are copyrighted, the other recipes are from our copyrighted books and any new recipes are studies for either books or TV shows. I just don't have time for additional ones and a stock recipe for charity cookbooks would be of little interest. I hope you will understand and forgive; a recipe that is any good takes a while to build, so I am not overflowing with them by any manner of means."

HENRY KISSINGER: "Regrettably, Mr. Kissinger's exhaustive schedule prevents him from honoring your request. He does appreciate, however, that you have thought to include him in your cookbook."

PAUL MCCARTNEY: "I regret to advise you that because he is a strict vegetarian, Paul only contributes to vegetarian cookbooks."

JACK LEMMON: "As much as Mr. Lemmon can appreciate your efforts in compiling this cookbook, it is our policy not to contribute to any publication."

MICKEY ROONEY: "Unfortunately, due to previous commitments, Mickey will not be able to participate (in your cookbook) at this time."

CARLOS SANTANA: "As Carlos' interests do not

take him to the kitchen very often to prepare food, he cannot contribute a recipe."

PIERRE TRUDEAU: "Mr. Trudeau has asked me to explain to correspondents that he continues to receive such a volume of letters and of telephone calls that he finds it very difficult to concentrate on the things he planned for his retirement. Consequently, Mr. Trudeau will not be answering his mail or taking telephone calls for an undetermined period of time."

ANOTHER LETTER from Buckingham Palace (Princess Fergie): The Princess Royal has asked me to write and thank you for your letter. I very much regret that it is not possible for The Princess to help you in the way that you ask. As I am sure you will understand, Her Royal Highness receives many similar requests like this one each day. I am sorry to have to send you a disappointing answer."

THE PRESIDENT of France, Francois Mitterant was extremely nice in sending along a photograph of himself, but declined to send a recipe on the grounds that "he does not answer any personal questions" and my request for a recipe falls into the personal questions category.

FROM THE office of the President of the Philippines comes this note: "We regret to inform you that we cannot accommodate your request. At the risk of accommodating just a few and disappointing so many others, all requests for

contributions to books have been turned down as a general rule. Nevertheless, we send every good wish for the success of your project."